HOPE AMONG US

Stories of Three Young Cancer Survivors

Rhonda Eyzaguirre PhD
Jennifer Dresser
Mari Guzman

DEDICATION

To my husband Jorge,
for being my rock and caregiver every step of the way.
To my mother Jane,
for inspiring me as a fellow author and breast cancer survivor.
To my children Mateo and Raquel,
for their sweetness and resilience at every turn.
And to my friends, family and fellow survivors,
for carrying me through the darkness with their love and light.

-Rhonda Eyzaguirre PhD

To my husband Jeff,
for his sensitivity, love, and dedication to me and our children.
To my children Jeffrey, Jordan, Juliana, and Jillian,
for giving me motivation to continue to fight.
And to my parents, siblings, in-laws,
extended family, and friends,
for helping us through our most difficult times.

-Jennifer Dresser

To my husband and best friend Elias,
I love you whether times are good or bad, happy or sad. We are
better together.
To my children Carina, Andy, and Marco,
I love you all to the moon and back.
To my sister Juani and my nephews Alex and Carlos,
without whose support I could not have battled the dark days.
To my faith keepers, thank you for keeping the faith for me when
I could not find it within myself.

-Mari Guzman

CONTENTS

Part IV
INTERVIEWS

Part V
SURVIVORSHIP & RESOURCES

FOREWORD

When I started practicing medicine, I had no idea how my life would be impacted by the profession I chose. The relationships and even friendships I have developed over the years with so many of my patients make me humble and full of gratitude. Breast health, especially breast cancer, is an intimate topic and I am honored to have so many patients allow me into their lives. The authors of this book are three of those patients, and I remember each of them distinctly, as I do nearly all my patients. Friends before their diagnoses, their lives become intertwined and their friendships grow deeper through a journey that none of them would have chosen.

This is the story of three amazing women who, when faced with cancer, overcame it with strength, hope and even humor. Told with such raw candor and emotion, their stories read like a fictional novel at times. I had to remind myself that these are real women with real stories which interestingly are told from different perspectives. First their own, including before, during and after their diagnoses. Second through the lenses of their loved ones, including their mothers, all of whom are breast cancer survivors themselves. I found their perspective particularly poignant, as family members are very much impacted by a cancer diagnosis, a fact often neglected by healthcare providers. This is one of the many insights I will take away from reading this book.

So many variables play a role in one's unique path through this devastating disease. However, the one thread that binds these women and so many cancer survivors is hope: hope to move forward and beyond cancer, hope for their own future and those of their loved ones, and hope for other survivors, that they also may find strength and courage to face cancer with optimism and resilience.

This is the Hope Among Us.

Claudia De Young MD; MSc

INTRODUCTION

The evolution of this book came about due to several major life events among the three authors. These events were the authors enrolling their children in the same classes, their shared experience as breast cancer survivors, and the challenges created by the COVID-19 pandemic. Rhonda and Mari met more than nine years ago when their sons started preschool in the same class. Rhonda and Jennifer met more than five years ago when their daughters started kindergarten together. They have become friends through their children and have many shared experiences, including their diagnoses of breast cancer.

Interestingly, all three authors were diagnosed with the same kind of breast cancer, estrogen progesterone positive (ER+ PR+), HER2 negative (HER2-) invasive ductal carcinoma (IDC). They were all diagnosed at the same hospital at a young age. Also, their mothers are all breast cancer survivors.

Despite the similarities in their experiences, the authors have different time periods of survivorship. Jennifer was diagnosed at age 37 in 2012 and had a recurrence in 2019. She recently completed her second active treatment phase in

June 2020. Rhonda was diagnosed with breast cancer at age 38 in 2017 and completed active treatment in May 2018. Mari was diagnosed at age 42 in 2019, and recently completed active treatment in November 2020.

During 2020, as the authors met with each other to provide support and encouragement for their cancer treatments, they decided to document their tumultuous breast cancer journeys. Despite the challenges of cancer and COVID-19, their experiences all underscored a similar message of hope. A working definition of hope that resonates with the authors is an optimistic state of mind despite difficult events in one's life or in the world. Philosopher and author G.K. Chesterton elaborated, "Hope is the power of being cheerful in circumstances that we know to be desperate." According to Ernest Rosenbaum, M.D., and David Spiegel, M.D., heads of the Stanford Center for Integrative Medicine and authors of the article *Hope as a Strategy*, "Survivors are well advised to hope for the best but prepare for the worst. They can live with hope for a cure, a remission, or stable cancer without suffering and enjoy high quality of life with family and friends for as long as possible." They also explain that, "The hope is to be kept alive, to live, and to recover through a resilient attitude rather than a feeling of despair. Hope is often a shared feeling with one's personal team of family and friends because the future is often nebulous. Hope keeps one alive to fight for another day, a month, a year, and a return to better health."

Through this optimistic and inspirational lens of hope, the authors share their unique perspectives while exploring their experiences battling breast cancer. The authors present their experiences through different lenses of time (one month, six months, and three years in survivorship). They share raw, honest accounts of their breast cancer journeys amid challenges such as multiple tumors, a recurrence, and multiple positive lymph nodes. Also, in the past few years, several of their close friends in their late thirties and early forties have been diagnosed with cancer. Their stories form a tapestry amid the struggles of cancer during COVID-19, all while echoing a consistent message of hope.

The authors' stories of hope and triumph are told in five chronological parts: (I) Our Lives Before Cancer, (II) Our Diagnoses, (III) Treatment, (IV) Interviews, and (V) Survivorship and Resources. Part I, Our Lives Before Cancer, introduces the authors' personal backgrounds and shares key experiences from their lives before cancer. It focuses on major life events, family composition and medical history that help form their backstories. Part II, Our Diagnoses, recounts in detail each author's specific experience of receiving a breast cancer diagnosis and her decision-making process. Part III, Treatment, covers their treatments, including chemotherapy, radiation, surgeries, and hormone therapy. One of Jennifer's surgeries, and part of Mari's chemotherapy, radiation, and surgeries, occurred during COVID-19, which greatly impacted the experience of their treatments. Part IV, Interviews, explores the authors' breast cancer diagnoses and treatment through the eyes of family members. The authors interviewed their mothers as breast cancer survivors to obtain their unique perspectives. They also interviewed their spouses and children, who spanned from age 7 to 22, to understand the experience of cancer from family members. The final part, Survivorship and Resources, addresses how the authors are navigating the survivorship phase and provides relevant resources. The first two chapters provide two unique lenses of survivorship (social or spiritual) that can be utilized to foster resilience in survivorship. Rhonda's two main survivorship programs coincided with COVID-19. The final two chapters conclude with recommended resources during treatment and final thoughts. The intended audience is breast cancer patients, cancer survivors, caregivers, medical providers, and anyone intrigued by the rise of breast cancer in young women.

PART I
OUR LIVES BEFORE CANCER

Life is like a roller coaster.
You can either scream every time
there is a bump in the road
or you can throw your hands up
and enjoy the ride.

Ben Busko

1

MEDICAL MYSTERIES

Rhonda's Life Before Cancer

I grew up as an only child in a picturesque neighborhood in the heart of San Francisco. I was blessed to attend a private Jewish elementary school while playing soccer, taking tap dance lessons, and traveling with my devoted parents. My parents provided me with a childhood that was stable and even idyllic—until the end of fifth grade.

In the summer of 1989, while my mother and I were visiting family in Kentucky, we received a phone call that changed my life forever. As I played ping-pong in the basement with my cousins, my mom called out to me. She told me that my father had died unexpectedly in the living room of our home. We were both in shock and rode to the airport the next morning in deafening silence. Our content family of three had suddenly become a broken and devastated family of two. My father died at the young age of 50 due to an unexplained sudden cardiac arrest. He was physically fit and had no medical issues, so his death came as a complete shock to everyone. My mother and I grieved for a long time and had a very difficult year.

In September, I switched from my small private elementary school to a large, urban middle school, where I witnessed many fights in the schoolyard. In October, the 1989 San Francisco earthquake shook my world (quite literally) a third time. I was at the lowest, darkest point of my young life. Luckily, I found a glimmer of light in a friendly classmate named Mindy who was also a tap dancer. She ultimately became my best friend, still brightens my world, and is my main confidant to this day. We both attended Lowell, a magnet high school with high academic standards. We were thrilled that we both got acceptance letters to the University of California, Berkeley.

While majoring in psychology and anthropology at Berkeley, I met my future husband during a summer job at a law firm in San Francisco. I was a law librarian and he worked in office services. Opposites attracted as I was shy, reserved and nerdy, while he was gregarious and hilarious—not to mention handsome. I continued working there throughout my senior year just to be near him. That same year, I applied to graduate programs in school psychology and chose U.C. Santa

Barbara. My new boyfriend was reluctant to relocate with me to Santa Barbara. Right before the big move, I changed course and stayed at UC Berkeley for graduate school. We lived in San Francisco and got married four years later.

That next summer we bought a house in Elk Grove. I also found a job as a school psychologist in a nearby school district where I have worked for the past fifteen years. My father's sudden death impacted my chosen profession of school psychologist. I wanted to help kids that were struggling with traumatic life events and life challenges. My dissertation topic was born from my early traumatic life experience and was entitled "Teachable Moments Around Death: An Exploratory Study of the Beliefs and Practices of Elementary School Teachers." I interviewed elementary school teachers about how they would handle various scenarios and potential teachable moments around death. After ten years at Berkeley, I graduated with a Ph.D. in school psychology.

With my dissertation completed, I was overjoyed to become pregnant a few months later. Due to my pre-existing conditions of kidney disease and high blood pressure, my pregnancy was considered high-risk, resulting in frequent ultrasounds and non-stress checks. Thankfully, my son was delivered full-term and without any complications. However, weeks later, I started having frequent bouts of sweating and shaking. I saw an endocrinologist who diagnosed me with hypoglycemia (low blood sugar) but could not determine the underlying cause. He attributed my extreme blood sugar fluctuations to breastfeeding. He instructed me to check my blood sugar several times a day and keep a daily food log. My blood sugar levels dropped to the 40s quite often, but no further testing was done, even though I had seizures and lost consciousness several times. When I requested an MRI, my endocrinologist told me that scans would not be done until I stopped breastfeeding. After 13 months, I stopped breastfeeding and was granted an MRI, which found a tumor at the head of my pancreas. In March 2009, I had a Whipple procedure, a complex six-hour surgery to remove the tumor along with the head of the pancreas, gallbladder, and part of the small intestine. I spent 14 days in the hospital with a feeding tube and lost more than 10 pounds. Thankfully, I did not have any major complications, but it took me three months to recover, which was especially challenging with a one-year-old.

My first personal experience with breast cancer was when my mother was diagnosed with stage 1 triple negative at age 71. She opted for a lumpectomy, chemo and radiation. She chose a more aggressive treatment approach despite being stage 1 because her cancer was triple negative. She also wanted to do everything possible to prevent a recurrence and continue being a grandmother. I was 32 and pregnant with my second child. My mom cohosted my baby shower at her house even though she had only recently finished chemo and was still undergoing radiation. Thankfully, she finished radiation earlier than expected, and was able to be there for my daughter's birth. She told me that she entertained my two-year-old son in the waiting room during my delivery by removing her wig. My mom recently celebrated her tenth anniversary of being cancer-free!

During this same pregnancy, I was diagnosed with placenta previa (placenta attached to the cervix). I was considered high-risk due to the placenta previa, as well as my pre-existing health conditions of hypertension and kidney disease. My doctor suggested an induction at 37 weeks, but I wanted my baby to develop as much as possible, so we compromised and scheduled the C-section for 38 weeks and two days. However, my water broke at exactly 38 weeks while I was eating dinner at BJ's restaurant. Thankfully, my mom, husband, and son rushed with me to the hospital. My daughter was delivered via emergency C-section. I lost a lot of blood and had dangerously low blood pressure. After hours of uncontrolled bleeding, I needed a catheter, a balloon in my uterus, and a blood transfusion. Although the delivery was traumatic, I was grateful that my daughter was born perfectly healthy. My body fully recovered from another serious medical ordeal. Little did I know at the time, my medical adventures were just beginning.

2

SOMEONE ALWAYS HAS IT WORSE

Jennifer's Life Before Cancer

I grew up in a small town in Idaho at a time when life seemed to be simple. Growing up in Idaho with five siblings, I had a lot of opportunities to learn how to work. At age twelve, to earn money in the summer, I started topping corn and hoeing beets for the local farmers. I believe hard labor helped teach me a strong work ethic and mental toughness at a young age.

I was raised in a very religious Christian home that tried to be "Christ-centered." We attended church every Sunday and I participated in weekly youth activity meetings. I learned about prayer, faith, and God's eternal plan at a very young age. Not knowing what challenges life had in store for me, I am grateful for this faith that I hold very dear. Part of this faith is the belief that we were spiritual beings that lived with God before this Earth life, and that we will live with Him again someday. This belief changes my perspective about this short earth life and death. In the grand scheme of eternity, this earth life is just a blink in time. It gives me great comfort to know that I will live with my family and God again after I have passed through mortality. This faith has sustained me in the darkest of times.

I have several great examples of positive people in my life, but two people stand out. One of them is my mother. I almost lost her when I was six years old due to a horrific car accident. One snowy December in 1981, she slid off an icy bridge and plummeted into a canal. She was in the ICU for over two months. The accident should have killed her or at least paralyzed her. I remember lying on my back on the hospital floor looking up at her, because her bed was flipped upside down to help prevent bed sores. She would have to write messages to me on paper, because her jaw was wired shut and she had a tracheotomy. She endured many surgeries, including having bolts drilled in her head to give her a metal halo with a back brace. Despite all of this, she always had gratitude, a smile, and a positive attitude. Thankfully, she made a full recovery. This made a great impression in my mind at a young age on how to handle adversity.

My other pillar of support is my sweet husband, whom I met while attending school at Brigham Young University. I was a bet between him and his BYU track teammate. They had a friendly wager on who would ask me out first. I am sure you can guess who won that bet. Ten months later, we were married and continued attending school. Following graduation, my husband got his first teaching job back in his home state of California. Shortly after moving to California, we started our family and have lived there ever since. We have been blessed with four healthy, amazing kids—two older sons and two younger daughters.

I have been blessed throughout my life; not to say that it's been perfect or without some challenges. These challenges include having to have my children via C-section, experiencing the disappointment of two miscarriages, and the joys and heartaches of motherhood. I have also witnessed a lot of tragedy throughout my life. In recent years I have had to painfully watch my brother-in-law and his devastated wife bury their beautiful two-month old son who died suddenly from SIDS. In addition to this heart-breaking event, a friend buried her 14-year-old special needs son due to drowning. Tragically, this was the second child she lost.

I have also recently experienced three people I care about die of metastatic breast cancer. My friend, Judy, was sixty-five years old and had been battling breast cancer for 10 years. She was a close family friend and had even thrown a bridal shower for me. My sister-in-law's mother, Janis, was seventy-three years old and lost a two-year battle to breast cancer that had metastasized to her brain. Most recently, my sweet friend Lucy lost her one-year battle to breast cancer after it metastasized to her bones. She was about as close to perfect as a person could possibly be. She was only forty-five years old and left behind an adoring husband and three beautiful children. I had been friends with her for twenty-two years. These are all heart-breaking events that have caused me great sadness. However, they have also made me appreciate my blessings more and not feel sorry for myself when I am having a bad day. There is always someone who has it worse.

3

BEFORE THE STORM

Mari's Life Before Cancer

My childhood was not a typical one. To understand my childhood, it is necessary to understand my roots. About eight years before I was born, my parents and eight-year-old sister, along with several members of my maternal family, immigrated to the United States from Spain. They, like so many others, came to this country in search of the American dream. Having lived their entire lives in a small village in the south of Spain under the dictatorship of Francisco Franco, they were seeking a better life for their family. They lived in a village where everyone lived off the land and bartered for their needs. Most homes did not have running water or electricity, and clothes were washed by hand. They worked extremely hard each day for everything they had, so making the decision to leave it all behind was not easy. They settled in a small town in Northern California, about an hour away from San Francisco.

To say that their transition from a small village in Spain to a small town in Northern California was challenging is an understatement. With no knowledge of the English language and a totally different way of life than what they were accustomed to, there were many struggles. But, as they did in Spain, through hard work and perseverance, my parents built a new and better life for themselves and my sister. My dad learned some English and acquired many skills that helped him become a successful real estate investor and manager. My sister adjusted quickly to the American school system and learned English, while my mother was the glue that held the family together. When the time was right, my parents decided to expand their family, and I was born in July of 1977.

Being the child of Spanish immigrants, I was immersed in Spanish culture and traditions. I grew up speaking Spanish, even though I did not always want to. I really had no choice, as my mother and most of my maternal family did not speak English. We were a very close-knit family, and I was very fortunate to live down the street from my grandparents, aunts, uncles, and cousins. But, when I was five years old, my sister graduated from high school and moved back to Spain to attend college. Though she visited every summer, I could not help but miss the family of four we once were. She always took care of me and helped my parents navigate language barriers. Her absence left a gaping hole in our family, which I tried hard to fill. So, at a very young age, I began helping my family by translating for them at the bank, grocery store, and doctors' offices.

Growing up I excelled in school and became very self-sufficient, since my parents could not help me with homework and other school projects. I credit learning English to watching Sesame Street. My parents did, however, always provide me with a very loving home environment and instilled the values of hard work and perseverance in me. Those values provided me with the foundation that allowed me to attend the University of California, Davis, where I majored in sociology, with an emphasis on law and society, and Spanish. After completing my undergraduate studies in 1999, my passion for helping others impacted my decision to attend law school at McGeorge School of Law in the fall of 2000.

I met my future husband my second year of law school. We had several classes together and we were immediately drawn to each other. We became great friends before our friendship blossomed into a romantic relationship. I knew he was the man I wanted to marry when he stood by my side during one of the most difficult times of my life—when my mother was diagnosed with breast cancer. We had been going out for only a few months when I received the devastating news. She had stage 1 ductal carcinoma in situ and her tumor was estrogen and progesterone positive. She was only 57 years old at the time of her diagnosis, so she opted for a single mastectomy to prevent a recurrence. She also had reconstructive surgery. I attended each one of her medical appointments and surgeries. I translated for her as I had always done and provided emotional support for her and my father. Being the glue that holds our family together, I am so grateful that my mom has been cancer free for 17 years.

I graduated from law school in the spring of 2003 and took the California bar exam that summer. I was lucky to pass the exam my first time and found a legal job in the Sacramento area. Shortly thereafter, I became engaged and bought my first home. We had been engaged for about a year when I received some devastating news once again. My fiancé had gone to the doctor for a routine exam and the doctor discovered a lump in his neck. That lump turned out to be papillary thyroid cancer. He had multiple surgeries to remove his thyroid and underwent radioactive iodine treatment. His doctor assured us this was one of the most curable forms of cancer and that the risk of recurrence was low.

We went on with our lives and were married in August of 2006. We had our first son in July of 2008. Life was busy working as attorneys and raising our family, and the thought of cancer striking our family again was the furthest thing from our minds. In the summer of 2011, we decided to expand our family. My son was three years old and we felt the time was right for another child. However, our plan was quickly thwarted after my husband went in for a cancer follow-up appointment. His endocrinologist ordered annual ultrasound scans of his neck, and the latest imaging revealed suspicious lymph nodes in his neck, so a biopsy was performed. A few days later we received devastating news. The biopsy results had a preliminary diagnosis of anaplastic thyroid cancer. This type of cancer is one of the fastest growing and most aggressive of all cancers, and the survival rate is very low. To say that we were in a state of shock is an understatement. We spent the next three weeks attending various medical appointments and preparing for major surgery, a radical neck dissection. The day of surgery arrived and members of both of our families were at the hospital to support us. We all sat nervously in the hospital waiting room for hours while my husband underwent surgery. After what seemed like an eternity, the surgeon appeared and shared some very good news with us. During the surgery tissue samples were sent to pathology, which confirmed that the cancer was papillary thyroid cancer, not anaplastic thyroid cancer. Thankfully, my husband's cancer was curable after all. In that moment I felt as though the weight of the world had been lifted off my shoulders. We all shed tears of joy and jumped with excitement. The memory of that day remains vivid even today.

Unfortunately, my husband's initial terminal diagnosis inflicted long-lasting emotional trauma on me. I spent years in therapy working on healing from the trauma and learning how to navigate the difficult aftermath of a cancer recurrence. However, the thought of another cancer recurrence eventually planted itself in my distant memory, and our lives mostly returned to normal. At that point, we expanded our family with our second son, who was born in February of 2013. Although life was chaotic with two active boys and demanding careers, we were just thankful to be healthy and thriving. But despite having various personal experiences of loved ones with cancer, nothing could have prepared me for my own breast cancer diagnosis.

PART II
OUR DIAGNOSES

You never know how strong you are
until being strong is the only choice you have.

Bob Marley

4
MEXICO TO A MUTATION
Rhonda's Diagnosis

I always tried to follow healthy habits. I exercised at the gym regularly, was assistant coach for my daughter's soccer team, and maintained a healthy BMI. I cooked well-balanced meals and generally avoided junk food (although I have a sweet tooth). I also did not smoke or do drugs, and rarely drank alcohol. I was under the assumption that I was young and healthy, and therefore at low risk for developing breast cancer.

However, toward the end of 2016, at age 38, I felt a lump in the middle of my right breast. It seemed to get bigger when I was having PMS symptoms and would then seem to disappear shortly after my period. On New Year's Day in 2017, I emailed my primary care doctor about my concerns and asked if I should have an ultrasound, particularly because my mother was a breast cancer survivor. He responded to my email the next day that I did not need to have a mammogram until I turned 40. Little did I know, he passed away unexpectedly less than a week later. His death was particularly shocking because he was only 39 years old and had one-year-old twins. In early March, I decided to have the lump examined and made an appointment with my new primary care doctor. I told her about the disappearing and reappearing lump. She felt it and immediately referred me for a biopsy the next day.

The next day, I met with Dr. DeYoung who performed the breast biopsy. I found out later that Dr. DeYoung not only works at the breast clinic in the surgery department, but also oversees the Breast Cancer Survivorship Program. During the biopsy appointment, she was quite knowledgeable but was also incredibly kind and compassionate. She immediately put me at ease and seemed genuinely interested in me as a whole person. The biopsy instrument was loud and painful, but the procedure was relatively quick. My mind was consumed about the test results, and it was very difficult to concentrate or think of anything else that weekend.

On Monday morning, March 13, 2017, I was sitting at my desk at work when Dr. DeYoung called on my cell phone. She was friendly at first but then abruptly asked me, "Why are you at work?" I did not know how to answer that question but thought to myself, *Where else I would be on a Monday morning?* She kindly suggested that I go to a quiet place without people around me. I hurriedly walked down the administration office hallway and out the side door. I stood outside of my office building and listened to Dr. DeYoung tell me that I had breast cancer. Even though I had had the biopsy, I was not expecting this earth-shattering news at all. She said that the next steps would be an ultrasound and then a mammogram. She did not yet know the stage or specific treatment. She recommended that I take one step at a time, which was very sage advice. She said that this was a bump in the road of my life and helped me process the news.

As she gave me some of the details, the passing period bell rang. I stood frozen as more than 2,000 high school students scurried across campus to their next classes. I continued listening to her, trying to comprehend foreign medical terms and commit new terminology to memory. I was transported back to the shock of the phone call as an eleven-year-old that my father had died. I went to the staff lounge and called my husband, who was supportive but also clearly blindsided. Then I called my mom, who had experienced a cancer diagnosis herself, but never as a mother wanting to protect her only child. These phone calls felt surreal, like I was telling a story about someone else. I was in a state of disbelief and could not fully grasp the devastating news I was sharing with them.

The next day I had an ultrasound of my breasts. I also

had my first and only mammogram of my life (I did not know this at the time). I was consumed by appointments and phone calls (bless Kaiser's swift response). My mind was consumed with a barrage of questions, such as the results of the ultrasound, results of the mammogram, my stage, the size of the tumor, what kind of surgery I would have, what treatments after surgery, and how many weeks I would be off from work. Thankfully, that coming Friday was my last day of work before spring break. I had planned to go on a family vacation to Nuevo Vallarta, Mexico, with my husband, two children, and mother. This trip to an all-inclusive resort was going to be my kids' first time exploring a different country. My mother wanted me to cancel the trip, but I was adamant that we should still go. I did not know what stage I was at, and whether I would have another opportunity to take a family vacation for a while, or ever again.

Dr. DeYoung phoned me with ultrasound results which indicated a spot on the side of my right breast that looked suspicious, suggesting cancer in the lymph nodes. She shared that surgery would probably be the next step, after a one-hour consultation with the surgeon. She also summarized various treatment options and said that my case would be discussed by the tumor board the next day. On Friday, I had an additional biopsy, this time of the lymph nodes. I also had blood drawn for genetic testing due to my mother's history of breast cancer. In addition, I was scheduled for a positron emission tomography (PET) scan at nuclear medicine the day before the trip. A PET scan uses a mildly radioactive drug to show areas of your body where cells are more active than normal. It can help to find out where and whether the cancer has spread.

Before PET scan, I was told to prep in the following ways: follow a high protein, no-carb diet two days before the procedure (kind of hard); avoid alcohol, tobacco, and exercise (not hard at all); and do not bring children, jewelry, or valuables with me (more of a relief, actually). For the appointment, I brought a portable water bottle to stay hydrated, and used visualization techniques. It was a long appointment, but less intimidating than I expected. It would take several days to get the results of the PET scan, so I decided to take the trip to Mexico.

The resort in Nuevo Vallarta was a welcome escape, a tropical paradise with delicious never-ending food and drinks, multiple pools, lush gardens, and expansive balconies with ocean views. I saw my six-year-old daughter boogie board for the first time, and my son swim up to the bar to order bottomless tropical smoothies. We swam with dolphins and lounged in a rooftop pool. Despite my extreme uncertainty about my health and our family's future, these experiences created joyous memories of our family that are etched in my mind to this day.

A few days after I returned from Mexico, I received the

results from the PET scan. Thankfully, the cancer was contained in the right breast area, and had not spread beyond the lymph nodes.

Additional results from the biopsy revealed that I had invasive ductal carcinoma, which meant that my cancer began growing in a milk duct and had invaded tissue of the breast outside of the duct. The tumor was estrogen and progesterone positive (ER+, PR+) and HER2 negative (HER2-). HER2 is a protein called human epidermal growth factor receptor 2 and it promotes the growth of cancer cells. Because I was HER2 negative, my breast cancer was not fueled by this protein, but I was ER+ and PR+. Estrogen and progesterone are hormones that help regulate a woman's menstrual cycle and play an important role in pregnancy. Thus, my breast cancer was primarily fueled by these hormones.

Next, I met with the surgeon, who had also conducted my Whipple procedure eight years prior! He seemed quite surprised to see me again in my 30s, and for an entirely different reason. I was reassured since he knew my medical history and had already operated on me. With the encouraging PET scan results and a familiar surgeon, I became more optimistic about my health and my future. Regarding the surgery options between lumpectomy and mastectomy, I was advised to do a mastectomy because of the size of the tumor, and because a lumpectomy would not lead to a good cosmetic outcome. There were also options of implants or using my own tissue. Some candidates can have immediate reconstruction, but I would be having delayed reconstruction due to the need for tissue expanders (to stretch the skin) and radiation.

The morning before my surgery, I received a call about my genetic test results. The geneticist explained that I had no mutations on 25 different genes associated with an increased risk of cancer but had a Variant of Uncertain Significance (VUS) on my BRCA2 gene. For BRCA1/2 carriers, the chance of breast cancer on the other side ten years after initial diagnosis is about 10-30 percent compared to 5-10 percent for survivors without a mutation. Also, the lifetime risk of a cancer on the other side is 40-65 percent for BRCA1/2 carriers. According to the Genetics Home Reference of the National Institutes of Health, "Sometimes, genes thought to be related to a particular genetic condition have mutations, but whether these changes are involved in development of the condition has not been determined; these genetic changes are known as Variants of Unknown Significance (VUS)." Thus, I had a certain mutation (specifically, p.13103M) on a cancer-causing gene (BRCA2), but it was unknown if this mutation was linked to cancer or was harmless. The geneticist at Kaiser said that most variants turn out to be normal human variation, but there was not enough data to know at that time. She recommended that I ask my family members to get tested. She also recommended that I stay in contact for three to five years to see if the mutation gets reclassified.

Despite the uncertainty of this genetic finding, the news changed my desired treatment plan for surgery. I knew that I wanted a bilateral mastectomy to reduce my risk of getting cancer on the unaffected side. I called and requested the bilateral mastectomy but was informed that the hospital only had time on the operating room schedule for a unilateral. I was given the choice to have a single mastectomy the next day or delay the surgery altogether. Both options were unacceptable to me. I requested that they find room on their operating schedule for both sides. Later that day I received the call that made me nervous, petrified, and grateful all at once. I would have the bilateral mastectomy the next day.

5
NEVER A CAVITY
Jennifer's Diagnosis

I have never had a cavity, just breast cancer. Twice. I know this sounds a bit sardonic, but it is true. My whole life I had been free of any major illness or disease, including my oral health—not even a cavity. I have always strived to be healthy. I have eaten a healthy diet, always exercised, and been physically active. I have even lived a strict health code of no alcohol, no smoking, and no drugs throughout my life. I had done everything correct by the book. To feel like my body betrayed me is a bit of an understatement.

Imagine my shock when I was first diagnosed with breast cancer at 37 years old. In 2012 I was a wife and a mother of four young children. My youngest was two-and-a half. I had breastfed all four of my children (another protection against breast cancer) until they were at least 18 months old. I remember thinking, "Well, I have been done breast-feeding for about a year, so it would probably be good to start self-breast exams and at least get a baseline." I hadn't done self-exams before, because I was young and seemed to always be breast feeding—and you know how lumpy and bumpy your breasts can be with that.

I don't believe it's a coincidence that I just randomly had the thought to start self-exams, because the first time I did it in the shower, I found a lump. A little hard nodule, like a small pea, on the outside perimeter of my left breast. I wasn't too concerned because I was only 37 years old. However, I did call my OB-GYN office and tell them about my new discovery. They asked me if I was menstruating, which I was, so they said to wait a couple of weeks and then call back if it was still there. I really wasn't too concerned, so I went about my daily life, giving little thought to it. I went to our church's girl camp as a counselor the following week and when I got home, I re-examined myself. The lump was still there, so my OB-GYN told me to come in. After he did a breast exam, he wasn't too concerned either, especially since I didn't have a family history of breast cancer and I was only 37 years old. He stated he wanted to err on the side of caution, so he ordered a mammogram for me.

The following day (yes, they were quick), I had my first mammogram. It was not pleasant, and a little concerning when they told me they were sending me over right then for an ultrasound. I remember looking at the screen as the sonographer took measurements and pictures to see if anything looked abnormal. As soon as the ultrasound ended, they asked if I could come back in an hour for a biopsy. One of the beauties of our health care organization is that everything is done "in-house" so you're not waiting long for tests. I hung around the hospital for the next hour and called my husband and mother to let them know I was having a biopsy done. My mother made me feel at ease by telling me that she had fibroids and that's what it probably was, so I shouldn't worry. At the end of the biopsy, they told me they would get the results in a couple of days. Then they handed me some pamphlets, one of which was on breast cancer. I remember thinking it was odd but didn't give too much thought about it.

Two days later I was in the kitchen cooking dinner. I still remember my exact spot when the phone rang. The doctor on the other end told me my biopsy results were in and they weren't good. I braced myself for the news by falling into my husband's lap. My doctor told me that I had invasive ductal carcinoma. Those words were a bit foreign to me, but I knew carcinoma meant cancer, and my world seemed to be crumbling as he spoke. I tried to remain calm and write down what he was telling me, but my husband and I were in utter shock. We just held each other and cried when I hung up the phone. Not knowing how far the cancer had spread was the scariest part. It was invasive, so how far had it traveled?

Any time I am faced with big decisions, and this one felt like life or death, I take it to the Lord. I had never prayed so hard and sincerely in all my life. All I could think about was my family. I want to be here to raise my beautiful children with my amazing husband. I want to witness my children get married and have families of their own. I want to be a grandma one day and spoil my grandkids with snuggles and kisses. I needed to make the right decisions concerning my treatment. I prayed for guidance before each doctor's appointment and that my doctors would be inspired with their advice. I did research and consulted with my father-in-law (a retired physician) regularly.

A week and a half later I had a lumpectomy with a sentinel lymph node biopsy (injecting blue dye to find the first lymph nodes closest to the tumor). The most painful part was before surgery, having a metal wire shoved into the side of my breast to "mark" the tumor. Three days after surgery I was given some good news; they removed three lymph nodes, none of which had cancer. Whew! That was a huge relief. However, the surgeon said the pathologist was a little perplexed about my margins due to the fact my tumor was growing in a bed of cancer (ductal carcinoma in situ, or DCIS). The surgeon advised me to just do radiation now. I told her I had four young children, so I was willing to do anything. If that meant mastectomy, I would do it. Her response was a bit alarming as she said a mastectomy was not necessary and that she could "keep me beautiful." Really?! I didn't care about beauty; my focus was on being here long-term for my family.

At this point in time a friend put me in contact with a breast cancer mentor, Ellie. Ellie was older but had gone through breast cancer twice and attended seminars with medical professionals to get the latest studies and treatments. She was a wealth of knowledge and helped me to better understand the disease I was fighting, as well as know what tests to request. A week and a half later I met with my oncologist. At the time he was the chief oncologist, so I felt I was in good hands. He didn't think any more surgery was necessary and ordered a consultation with the radiation oncologist. Due to Ellie's insight, I told my oncologist I wanted to get an MRI of my breasts (to make sure there wasn't something lurking that the mammogram didn't pick up). I also requested an Oncotype DX test. The oncotype test was not standard at the time and was very expensive. He told me if he ordered the test, I would have to agree to take tamoxifen (hormone therapy drug) for five years.

My genetics test came back negative for BRCA 1 and 2. I was relieved because that meant I could keep my ovaries. My MRI came back and wasn't showing anything new. However, my oncotype test came back a little more concerning. My recurrence score was a 24. At the time this was the "intermediate group." The low group was up to 18 and didn't benefit from chemo. For my group, the intermediate group (19-30), it was not clear at the time if you benefited from chemo. My oncologist didn't think the benefits of chemo outweighed the risks, so he advised me against chemo. I really struggled, because I wanted to make the right decision and with there not being enough data and so much uncertainty, I didn't feel at peace. I received a second opinion from another oncologist who agreed to not do chemo. Due to their advice, I ruled out chemo. I was now faced with the decision to do radiation or a mastectomy.

I met with the radiation oncologist and had concerns. In a nutshell, she told me that a minimal amount of radiation would go to the heart and lungs, but they couldn't guarantee that no damage would be done. Secondary cancers were also discussed. I did some research online and found a doctor talking about breast reconstruction being more difficult after radiation. I got a second opinion from another radiation oncologist. I told him to be candid with me and to advise me as if I were his sister. His advice was to do the mastectomy, maybe bilateral, since I was so young. I left that consultation crying, because I knew what I needed to do.

6

NOT SO HAPPY ANNIVERSARY

Mari's Diagnosis

August 26 is a very special day. It is the day I married my best friend in 2006. When I woke up on this day in 2019 it was going to be a great day. Even though it was a dreaded Monday and I had to work, my husband and I had a fun evening planned. Dinner with the kids at one of our favorite restaurants, and we would end the night with a slice of our favorite cake and a glass of champagne. Before the fun was set to begin, I had to make it through the workday. I dashed out the door with the hope that traffic would be light. Of course, it was not; the normal 20-minute drive took two hours due to an accident. But the sun was shining, and I was listening to my favorite country music station. There was even an advertisement for an upcoming concert that I wanted to attend. I was about to call my husband to tell him we should buy tickets when I felt a stabbing pain in my left breast. It was a pain I had never felt before. It came and went very quickly, but the pain was severe enough that I felt the need to do a breast self-exam. So right there in the middle of traffic I started to feel my breast. And to my surprise I felt a lump, about the size of a pea, near my nipple. I kept feeling it in disbelief. Could this be a lump in my breast? Or was I just imagining it? I had my annual mammogram in January and nothing suspicious was found. I kept telling myself it was probably nothing. I went about my busy workday trying to forget about the lump, but that was impossible to do. Every hour or so I would feel my breast; sometimes I felt the lump and other times I did not. I thought I was losing my mind. I was anxious to get home that day so that my husband could feel my breast and tell me that I was just imagining the lump. And then we could go about our anniversary plans. As soon as I got home, I rushed into the bedroom with my husband. I told him what I thought I had found and asked him to feel my breast. He too thought it was all in my head at first. As he was feeling my breast, I saw the expression on his face change from happy to serious. He was feeling the lump I had felt and there was something there. As we both examined my breast further, we noticed a small dimple on my nipple. I had never noticed this dimple before, but truth be told, I had never examined my breast so closely. I had a very bad feeling about this. I knew that I needed to see a doctor right away. I immediately called my health insurance appointment line. I spoke with an advice nurse who agreed I should be seen. Fortunately, an appointment was available the very next morning in the breast clinic. We scrapped our dinner plans and just picked up takeout. The thought of celebrating our anniversary just did not seem right.

After a long night with very little sleep and a lot of worry, the morning came, and it was time to get ready for my appointment. My husband wanted to accompany me, but oddly enough, this was something I wanted to do alone. Looking back, I think the thought of having my husband go to the appointment made the situation more serious. I was trying to convince him, and more importantly myself, that the lump I had found was nothing serious. He agreed to let me go alone on the condition that I would update him as soon as my appointment was over. So alone I went, and I regretted every second of that decision as I sat nervously in the waiting room of the surgery department where the breast clinic was located. After what seemed like an eternity, the nurse called my name and led me to a room. When the doctor walked in, I was visibly anxious. My hands were shaking, and I was sweating profusely. She had only been in the room for a few seconds when tears started to stream down my face. I told her that I had found a lump in my breast and a dimple on my nipple. I was embarrassed to tell her that I had only noticed them for the first time yesterday, but I did. Even though my mother was a 17-year breast cancer survivor, I was not very good about doing monthly self-breast exams. Unfortunately, I was that person who was lulled into a false sense of security from a normal mammogram only seven months prior. The doctor assured me that I had done the right thing by making an appointment right away. As she examined my breast, she immediately felt the lump and acknowledged the dimple. She then brought in an ultrasound machine and further examined my breast. She proceeded to tell me that she was very concerned with her findings and felt it was necessary to refer me for a mammogram and biopsy. Tears started to stream down my face again. She was very compassionate and tried to comfort me with words of hope and encouragement. She had an excellent bedside manner and truly made me feel like I was in great hands. She was able to get me an appointment on Thursday morning, so I would have to wait a few days.

As promised, I called my husband immediately after the appointment to let him know how it had gone. He could tell by my trembling voice that something was wrong. He could hardly understand the words that were coming out of my mouth. I just remember him telling me over and over to take a deep breath. I finally blurted out that the doctor was very concerned, and that a biopsy of the lump was necessary. After a few minutes of silence, he calmly told me that we were in this together and that he was going to be with me every step of the way. The next couple of days oddly flew by. It was a very busy time for me at work, but it was a welcome distraction. I needed something to consume my mind other than the fear and worry of what was to come next. Before I knew it, the morning of my appointment had arrived. This time, it was a given that my husband would be going with me, having regretted going alone to my last appointment. We both sat nervously in the waiting room of the radiology department. When the nurse called my name, I went in for the mammogram by myself. My husband waited patiently, hoping that a biopsy would not be necessary after all. Unfortunately, that was not the case. The lump found on the mammogram was very concerning and would have to be biopsied. The nurse called my husband back and allowed him to go with me to the room where the biopsy would take place. The radiologist and a technician walked in and began to inform me about the procedure. I started to sob and hyperventilate. A nurse was called in to assist and she was amazing. She held my hand and rubbed my back. They offered to postpone the biopsy because I was so emotional. Though I was terrified of moving forward, I knew that it was necessary that the biopsy be done right away. I lay down and they proceeded with the biopsy. It was very painful and there was a loud clicking sound, but it was over before I knew it. I quietly cried the entire time. My husband sat on a chair in the corner of the room, but it seemed as though he were a thousand miles away. It was hard to believe that just a few days prior I was getting ready to celebrate my 13ᵗʰ wedding anniversary and a wonderful future with my family, and now, I could not stop thinking about how that future was not guaranteed.

When the biopsy was complete, the radiologist discussed her findings with us. There was a three-centimeter mass in my left breast and one enlarged lymph node. She proceeded to tell us that her findings were highly suspicious for breast cancer, and she even began to talk about next steps, like a referral to the surgery and oncology departments. I was in disbelief. How could it be possible that I had a three-centimeter mass and an enlarged lymph node when only seven months prior my mammogram was normal? The biopsy results would likely take one or two business days and so I had to wait again. At that moment, the fear was paralyzing and all-consuming. The room felt cold and I just wanted to get out of there as quickly as possible.

I decided that I could not work while waiting for my biopsy results. I could not think clearly and needed time to process the information the radiologist had shared with me. My husband and I agreed that I should take a few days off work. I had not informed my boss of what was going on, other than needing a few hours off here and there for some medical appointments. I knew I was not legally obligated to share any information with him, but that afternoon after my biopsy I told my boss everything. I told him that I had a very concerning lump in my breast that was very likely breast cancer. It was very awkward to share such personal information, especially with a male boss, but after telling him, it felt as though some weight had been lifted from my shoulders. For the first time, maybe ever, I was making my health, both physical and mental, a priority. I do not think I will ever forget the look of shock on his face, and thankfully, he was very supportive of my request for time off.

After I left work, I drove straight home. I usually enjoyed the rare occasion when I had the house all to myself while my boys were at school and my husband was at work, but not on this day. The quiet seemed so loud and scary. I knew that I did not want to be alone with my thoughts. I decided to call my dear friend who was a stay-at-home mom. She is someone I can always count on, and this day was no exception. I had not had the opportunity to let her know what was going on until now. It was all happening so fast. She immediately invited me over to her home so that I would not be alone. And another dear friend joined us after her workday was over. We all have boys the same age and so much in common. Our lives have all been touched by cancer in one form or another, and I knew they could comfort me with their love and words of hope and encouragement. Time with my friends was just what my soul needed that afternoon.

One or two business days turned into four long days since it was Labor Day weekend. My two nephews were visiting from Spain and we had planned to spend the weekend together. They are in their twenties and visit often. But that was before I had found the lump in my breast. I was not sure that I could pretend as if nothing were wrong the entire weekend, and was hesitant to spend time with them. But I had already had numerous conversations with my sister who lives in Spain about what was happening. She encouraged me to also tell my nephews, so I did. They spent the weekend keeping me busy and filling my days with love and laughter. However, the nights were hard when I was alone with my thoughts. I barely slept that entire weekend.

When Tuesday came, it started off like any other Tuesday. I got my kids ready for school and saw my husband off to work. I had planned to go to breakfast with my friend to make the time pass a little faster. I barely had an appetite and did not feel like talking much. Both of those things are very out of character for me. But the company was nice and much needed. My husband and I had agreed that he would take the call from the radiologist. I did not feel strong enough to take the call myself. Every time my phone rang, I jumped out of my seat. There were a couple of false alarms during breakfast with my husband just calling to check on me. My friend did not want to leave me alone, but after breakfast, we agreed it was time for me to go home. I decided to run a quick errand. As I was driving down the street near my home, my phone rang. It was my husband. I knew this was the call that would change my life forever. I picked up the call and asked him if I should pull over. He said that would probably be a good idea. I could not hold back the tears and said, "It's cancer, isn't it?" He delivered the news that no husband should ever have to, but he did it with such grace and strength. He told me that I had a form of breast cancer called invasive ductal carcinoma (IDC). My lymph node was positive too. The radiologist had also informed him that this is the most diagnosed form of breast cancer, but that she did not have specific tumor markers yet. I had just become that dreaded statistic of being 1 in 8 women who are diagnosed with breast cancer in their lifetime. And it was devastating.

I learned some very important things in that week between finding the lump in my breast and my official breast cancer diagnosis. I gave myself permission to be worried, to be sad, and quiet, and crawl out of my skin, uncertain about what was next. Life can change in the blink of an eye, so never get too busy building a life that you forget to have one. And most importantly, embrace the love from others and do not be afraid to cry. These things do not make you weak. Allowing yourself to feel these things makes you strong. Finding a lump in your breast is not something any person wants. But, looking back, it was the first step in learning to live with a breast cancer diagnosis and the beginning of my cancer journey.

PART III
TREATMENT

A woman is like a tea bag;
you never know how strong it is
until it's in hot water.

Eleanor Roosevelt

7

DON'T LIVE LIFE WAITING FOR CANCER TO RETURN

Jennifer's Initial Treatment

After a couple of agonizing months of careful consideration, tons of research, and a lot of prayer, I decided to have a bilateral mastectomy. I was only 37 years old and I thought I would match better if both sides were done instead of having a single mastectomy. The idea of keeping my nipples was comforting, so I was willing to drive an hour-and-a-half to the Bay Area for doctors who were trained in performing "nipple sparing." At the time, there were no doctors in the Sacramento area who were doing this technique. Due to sagging breasts (thanks to breastfeeding), I was advised to first do a breast lift so my nipples would end up in their proper places after the bilateral mastectomy. This surgery itself was not painful, and the recovery took only a couple of weeks.

Three weeks later, right before Halloween, I had my double mastectomy. I was all smiles with my husband before going into surgery, but then reality hit me when I was rolled into the operating room. I remember lying on my back in the cold room with bright lights glaring in my face and sounds of the medical staff giving instructions to each other; I began to feel frightened. When the doctor asked me to state my name, birthdate, and declare the procedure I was having done, it hit me like a ton of bricks. With tears streaming down the sides of my face, it seemed surreal to say, "double mastectomy." I recall waking up feeling very nauseous and having difficulty breathing. There was an immense amount of pressure on my chest which prevented me from taking deep breaths. I was in the hospital for two days with a severe burning sensation and pressure in my chest. The expanders felt like hard plastic cups digging into raw, tender flesh. I was grateful to have the hospital bed to lower and raise to get up out of bed, since it was very difficult to move and use my arms. The drains sticking out of my back were uncomfortable and made it even more difficult to try to sleep on my back elevated. My drain output was normal, but my nipples were purple. I began to get fearful that one or both may "die." I was rather attached to these nipples because they were all that was left of "me," and were helping me deal with the trauma of the mastectomy.

Going in for my post-op appointment didn't help that anxiety when I started talking to another woman in the waiting room. She told me about her horrific experience with her mastectomy. My heart went out to her because she was on her second skin graft due to skin dying from her mastectomy. Poor woman, as if a mastectomy isn't traumatic enough. "There is always someone who has it worse."

I remember the first time I was able to take a shower post-surgery. The reality of it all hit me again, when I could not take in that amazing feeling of warm water hitting my chest. I do miss the feeling of a simple shower and having nerve sensitivity in that region, something I had taken for granted.

My appreciation and confirmation for my decision came when my surgeon called me with the pathology report. She told me that I had made the right decision, because there was ductal carcinoma in situ (DCIS) widespread throughout the entire breast. (So much for the MRI finding anything that might be "lurking.") She proceeded to tell me that she didn't think that radiation and tamoxifen would have taken care of it. This is the confirmation I needed to hear, because many of my doctors had advised me to do only a lumpectomy with radiation.

Two weeks after surgery, I was able to have my drains removed, and things were healing nicely. The burning and pressure in my chest were getting better with each passing week. The challenge was to not use my arms. I had four kids I was incapable of caring for, in addition to myself. However, the outpouring of love and support was beyond overwhelming. My kids would excitedly go to the door each evening to see what yummy dinner our church members were bringing that night. In addition to meals, women and friends from our church would show up to vacuum and clean the house. This was truly heaven sent and they were our angels. I recall one of the times soon after surgery that some of my friends showed up to clean the house, and one of them offered to wash my hair for me. I was unable to do this simple task at the time, and it needed to be done so desperately. These amazing selfless acts of service will forever stay in my mind and heart.

My reconstruction surgery, about six months later in the spring, went rather smoothly. I was very excited to get the hard, uncomfortable expanders out and my silicone implants put in their place. I ended up not needing drains for this exchange, and the recovery was not bad. I felt pretty good after a couple of weeks.

It was at about this time that my 73-year-old mother, who lives in the same town as me, received some scary news. During a routine mammogram they told her they needed to do a biopsy. A few days later her doctor called her and asked if she could come in. She learned she had estrogen positive invasive ductal carcinoma. Thankfully, the tumor was small and had not spread. After considering all her options, she decided to do a lumpectomy. Due to her age, she chose not to do radiation, and due to osteoporosis, she opted not to do any hormone treatments. She told me that she would die of something else before breast cancer killed her. This was her personal decision and one I respect.

I was still perplexed as to why I got cancer, and my oncologist's stunning response to it all was, "Shit happens." Not satisfied with this answer, I found a naturopathic oncologist in Arizona. He reviewed my files and told me that my tumor location (armpit) was highly suspicious. He educated me about the "Knick Theory." There are a great number of tumors and incidences of breast cancer in the upper outer quadrant of the breast near the armpit. The Knick Theory suggests that shaving creates abrasions or nicks in the skin, and then we apply anti-perspirant or deodorant, causing aluminum or parabens to enter our bloodstream. This is when I learned about parabens and the role they play in mimicking estrogen in our endocrine systems. I then started using natural deodorants and threw out any makeup or beauty products that contained parabens.

I took tamoxifen and made lifestyle changes, such as eating a more plant-based diet. My oncologist was retiring, and his last advice to me was rather wise, but easier said than done; "Don't live life waiting for cancer to return."

TREATMENT

8

UNLUCKY THIRTEEN

Rhonda's Treatment

My first treatment was a bilateral mastectomy, which was coincidentally scheduled on the same day as my mother-in-law's 70th birthday. We dropped off our children at my mother-in-law's house that morning. I tried to reassure everyone that compared to my previous six-hour Whipple surgery and 14-day hospital stay, this experience was going to be much easier. Nonetheless, it was major surgery that involved a bilateral mastectomy, axillary lymph node dissection, and placement of tissue expanders. I am eternally grateful that I had talked to Jennifer about her breast cancer experience and bilateral mastectomy. She gave me the sage advice to inquire about and request a nipple sparing mastectomy. None of my health care providers had discussed this option, and I had not read about it anywhere either. I am grateful to Jennifer for giving me the insider knowledge to bring it up to my oncology surgeon. He agreed if my plastic surgeon agreed, and thankfully my nipples were not removed during surgery. I stayed overnight because I developed a severe itching reaction to a family of pain medications but was able to go home the next day. I was in a lot of pain for several weeks, but regular pain medication (that I wasn't allergic to) and the removal of drains over time helped tremendously.

The pathology report came back a few days later and revealed that I did not have one large tumor (which had been suspected on scans), but 13 small tumors. An unlucky 13 tumors! I was shocked and scared to have so many tumors. I had heard about people having two or maybe three tumors, but not 13! Despite the large number, I tried to remain hopeful because they were small (between 1 and 11 mm). No skin or muscle was involved. Also, the cancer had spread to three of the 19 lymph nodes that were removed. Two positive nodes were in my axilla (armpit area) and one was an intramammary lymph node. Based on the findings, I was diagnosed with invasive ductal carcinoma stage 2a. Chemotherapy was definite due to having at least one positive lymph node. Radiation was a possibility because I had three positive lymph nodes (one to three positive nodes is possible for radiation; four or more is definite for radiation). On top of all that news, I also was told that the margins were not clear, and that I would need to have an additional surgery to clear the margins after I was done with chemotherapy.

My second treatment, chemotherapy, was given in two phases. The first phase was every other week for four cycles. I was given the standard combination of Adriamycin and cyclophosphamide (AC), followed by the second phase of Taxol. I had the option to receive Taxol weekly for 12 weeks, or a larger dose every other week for eight weeks. I chose the larger dose every other week because I would be done a month sooner and have only four treatments instead of 12. I also hoped the second option would make it easier for me to return to work on time after summer break. I printed out monthly calendars and wrote in my chemo appointments, other appointments, and other activities. I crossed out each day, which provided me with a motivational tool of how much I had accomplished what was coming up next.

Chemotherapy started on May 4, 2017; May the 4th be with me (I'm not a Star Wars fan but my husband and son are)! My husband took me to every single one of my treatments and helped me tremendously, both physically and emotionally. He was a calming, problem-solving co-captain throughout the turbulent waters of my treatment. He drove me to every appointment and helped calm me when I was feeling anxious (which was every appointment). One of his other main tasks was assisting with my cooling caps. I learned about cooling caps from a fellow breast cancer survivor whom

I met at a surgery recovery class. She was young and had long, beautiful hair. I approached her after class and was amazed to learn that she had finished chemo only three months prior. She explained that she had used cooling caps to minimize her hair loss. According to the American Cancer Society, "Scalp hypothermia is cooling the scalp with ice packs or cooling caps (cold caps) for a period of time before, during and after each chemotherapy treatment to try to prevent or reduce hair loss." Before my chemo, the woman graciously lent me her four sets of cooling caps. She also visited me during my first chemo and helped me with the timing and nuances of using cooling caps.

I was able to use the four cooling caps throughout all my chemo sessions. My husband bought dry ice every other week the night before chemo. We stored everything in a big cooler and dragged it to my station in the infusion clinic. The first five minutes felt like I was dipping my head directly into a bucket of ice. It was intense pain, but my head soon became numb within a few minutes. After the initial shock of the first cap, I was able to tolerate the rest of the cap exchanges reasonably well. My husband and I rotated them every twenty minutes. For the Taxol treatments, I also wore mittens and slippers to prevent neuropathy (nerve damage). I bought three sets of cooling mittens and three sets of cooling slippers on Amazon. We numbered them and used my iPad to keep track of the staggered 20-minute rotations.

I developed several of the typical chemo side effects

from AC. I was very sensitive to light and developed headaches quite often. I developed a dull, metallic taste in my mouth. I also had frequent nausea and fatigue. The steroids made it difficult for me to sleep. I learned to avoid sunlight, spicy foods, heat, and other triggers the first few days after each chemo session. I tried to drink a lot of water to flush out the chemo from my system. I kept the blinds in my bedroom drawn to keep out the light and tried to nap and rest often.

I was able to go back to work at the end of July as planned, and endured my last few chemo treatments while working full-time. Thankfully, I had very few side effects on Taxol other than fatigue and hair loss. I had lost about 60% of my hair and wore a hair topper to add some fullness. My eyelashes and eyebrows were completely gone. I colored the eyebrows with pencil and was able to blend in at work reasonably well, although I was much paler than usual. I had much less energy and mental clarity. Thankfully, my friend of 15 years and daily carpool buddy, Christy, was very understanding about my situation and extremely compassionate. A fellow school psychologist and mother of three, we are close confidants and help each other tremendously. I finished chemo in mid-August and brought in chocolates and cupcakes for the staff. My kids helped me make and decorate a bright pink Last Day of Chemo sign. I was relieved and grateful to be done with the second part of my cancer journey.

While I underwent chemo, I had regular visits with my plastic surgeon. During surgery, I had tissue expanders placed to stretch my skin and prepare for implants. The expanders had to be gradually inflated over several months, which was a very uncomfortable and painful process. The skin was very tight and felt like a balloon was stretching it.

My third treatment was a right breast skin excision (lumpectomy) in early September in order to clear the margins. I had the same surgeon as the Whipple and mastectomy. The surgery lasted less than two hours and involved an excision of the skin where my tumor had been. My surgery and recovery were obviously much quicker than the bilateral mastectomy. I was tired from the procedure but took only four days off from work. Thankfully, the pathology report came back that the margins were clear!

A month later in October, I started my fourth treatment, radiation. I was able to drive myself to the late afternoon appointments right after work. Although having three positive lymph nodes is in the gray area for recommending radiation, I had many risk factors that indicated that radiation was very strongly recommended. Specifically, I had 13 tumors, was only 38 at diagnosis, had a Variant of Uncertain Significance (VUS) on my BRCA2, and had a family history of breast cancer. For my treatment plan, I was told that four areas would be radiated and that the sessions would be five days a week for six weeks. The most challenging part of radiation was holding still when my right arm was elevated above my head. My right arm felt heavy, and would become prickly, and then go numb. I remember closing my eyes and imagining that I was looking at the ocean. I made sure to use moisturizer and aloe creams on the radiated skin. I cut into the leaves of an aloe plant and scooped the aloe flesh, lathering it onto my skin every day. I also made sure to stay hydrated and tried to go to bed early throughout radiation. My skin held up well until the third to last day of radiation. I was prescribed silver sulfadiazine cream to lubricate the area and prevent further blistering. My skin looked like an inflamed sunburn but healed within a few weeks.

During the fall, I completed my fifth treatment, which was physical therapy. I was referred several months prior due to a tightness in my right arm that felt like a guitar string that was wound too tight. It ran from my armpit down to my elbow. My range of motion was significantly impaired, and has not returned to normal to this day. I received massages and learned stretches to help reduce the tightness and regain my shoulder motion. The physical therapist was very skilled technically, but also was able to connect with me emotionally. She asked genuinely caring questions about my cancer journey and my life beyond cancer.

In December, I began my sixth treatment, anti-estrogen medication. This was recommended because my tumors were estrogen and progesterone positive (ER+ PR+), meaning they were fueled by estrogen. I started leuprolide shots to suppress the production of estrogen in my ovaries. The shot was given every three months at the infusion clinic where I had gone for chemo. In conjunction with the Lupron shots, I was prescribed anastrozole to suppress any residual estrogen in my body. Anastrozole is a medication that given only to post-menopausal women. I was told that I would be taking anastrozole every day for at least five years, possibly ten. My side effects of chemically induced menopause and anastrozole included hot flashes, joint pain in my knees, and general stiffness whenever I woke up or sat in the same position for too long. The side effects lasted for several months, but lessened over time. I noticed that regular exercise (both cardio and strength training) and stretching helped greatly to reduce my side effects.

In March, I had my seventh and final treatment, which involved two surgeries on the same day. I had an implant exchange (tissue expanders exchanged for breast implants) and a bilateral salpingo-oophorectomy (removal of both ovaries and tubes). I was advised to have my ovaries removed as they are a main source of estrogen, which fuels my cancer, and I was at risk for ovarian cancer due to the VUS on my BRCA2. My plastic surgeon and OB-GYN needed to choose a date that worked for both providers and that gave my body enough time to heal from radiation. Interestingly, they chose March 13, the exact date of my diagnosis one year prior! I couldn't believe that a year had passed and that my final surgery would be on the exact same date I was diagnosed. March 13 was the day that my life pivoted, twice. After diagnosis day, everything appeared to be colored through the dark and uncertain lens of cancer. However, on surgery day one year later, March 13 marked a momentous end to treatment, including three surgeries, tissue expanders, chemo, radiation, and physical therapy. The three-hour surgery went well and without complications. I had completed a whirlwind year of treatment.

TREATMENT

9
TAKE TWO

Jennifer's Treatment for Recurrence

Once you have had breast cancer, knowing it is a chronic disease, it's rather difficult to put it out of your mind completely. About a year and a half after my mastectomy, I started noticing a lump on my incision scar where my original tumor was removed. I brought it up to my new oncologist, but he did not seem too concerned and said it was probably scar tissue or a suture tail left from the stitches. He advised me to monitor it over the next six months until I saw him again. Months later, I returned and brought up the lump again. He asked me if it had grown, but it really did not feel noticeably different. He referred me to a surgeon to have it biopsied. To my relief, the biopsy came back negative, so they deemed it scar tissue.

A few years later, in October of 2018, I started having pain down my left arm. The pain would sometimes radiate into my left hand. Some nights the pain was so severe that I could not sleep. I became concerned that my silicone implant had ruptured and was causing pain. I scheduled an appointment with a local plastic surgeon. He examined me and told me he did not think that the implant was compromised in any way. I asked if I could get an MRI, but he did not think it was necessary. He told me if the pain persisted then to call the office and we could schedule an MRI. I got busy with the holidays, as well as dealing with a kidney stone, so my focus was on other things. The pain in my arm was not constant but would come and go regularly.

After the holidays, I had some bad nights with the pain, so I called my mastectomy surgeon in the Bay Area and told her my concerns. She told me she wanted me to see a specific local surgeon in my healthcare network. The following week I met with a young bright surgeon and told her my concerns that I might have a ruptured implant. She said we could do an MRI, but that she was more concerned about the lump on my incision scar. I casually dismissed it and told her they did a biopsy on it in 2015 and deemed it scar tissue. She asked me if I felt confident that they got the right spot, because the surgeon's notes seemed to imply it was small and difficult to get the lump. She told me she wanted to do a biopsy right there in her office, just to be safe.

A couple of days later her nurse called me and said she had bad news. My heart sank; I began to have a lump in my throat, and every hair on my body was standing on end. She told me my biopsy tested positive for invasive ductal carcinoma. This time I knew exactly what that meant, and I had a wave of fear come over me. This time I did not have my husband's lap to fall into. I was home alone, so I fell to my knees and began to cry to the Lord. After minutes of sobbing and complaining to the Lord, I began to collect myself. I told the Lord I trusted in His plan for me, whatever that looked like, and I was putting everything into His hands. I just prayed that I would have the strength and courage to face whatever was going to come my way.

I was determined not to feel sorry for myself and to keep a positive attitude by focusing on the many blessings in my life. I made my husband promise me that no matter what, we would not get mad at God. No matter what was to come, we would keep the faith and trust in God's plan.

Within days I had an ultrasound and biopsy of my axillary area. I soon found out that it had spread to my lymph nodes. I knew that chemo was in my near future, but the most terrifying aspect was not knowing how far it had spread. Waiting for the PET scan results was the most painful and excruciating time. My mind would wander and thoughts of metastatic cancer to my bones or liver kept creeping in. I could tell it was equally painful for my poor husband. Once again, we held each other and cried when the results came back that there was no sign of metastasis other than in my chest wall and axillary area. My new oncologist, who specializes in breast cancer, told me to mentally prepare for a year to 18 months to complete my treatments and surgeries. I knew this was a mountain before me and I was going to climb it with strength not my own. "The journey of a thousand miles begins with one step," and I knew my Lord and family were going to be there every step of the way.

After my MRI came back showing there was a tumor near a major nerve bundle in my axillary area, my hospital's tumor board determined that I should do chemo first. Their thinking was that chemo may be able to shrink the tumor and that would help preserve the surrounding nerves during surgery. I attended a "chemo class" provided by my healthcare provider. During this class I learned about mouth rinses, proper eating during chemo, and to avoid the dentist. What?! I would have to skip my bi-annual cleaning?! You know me and my oral hygiene. . . I also turned to my next-door neighbor (who had recently gone through chemo) and Rhonda to discuss their experiences with chemo. We all handle stress differently. It's not a bad thing. For me, I am not a super private person. I need to talk about my problems, get educated, and seek advice so that I feel more in control and can better handle my challenges. It was very helpful to me to get perspectives from people who had recently gone through my same treatment plan, so I knew what to expect. Rhonda was a fantastic resource with so much information. She was also so generous in loaning me her mittens and booties for the ice therapy needed during chemo.

Days later I was off to radiology to get my port put in. They don't put you out, they just give you something to make you "comfortable." They showed me the port ahead of time and it looked so big and bulky. I asked if that was the "mini" (a smaller version that can be used in smaller women). It was not, so they replaced it with the mini. Looking back, I am so glad that I asked for the mini, because even that seemed big and was a little uncomfortable. It remained a bit sensitive during the months of chemo.

The following day I visited a well-respected hairdresser to get my long locks cut off. I had a hard time justifying spending so much money on a haircut only to lose my hair in a month; however, this was my opportunity to experiment with a cute short haircut. I came away with a darling haircut, but not one I would dare get under normal circumstances. Ultimately, I felt it would be less traumatic to lose my hair gradually—short pieces coming out rather than long strands.

I decided I was going to adopt an anthem for my treatment. Rachel Platten's "Fight Song" got me so jazzed every time I would hear it. My girls and I would sing it at the top of our lungs in the car when it would play on the radio. This song was going to be my anthem and I was going to listen to it throughout my treatments. This was my "get in the zone" and "kick cancer's butt" song.

On February 27, 2019, an hour before my scheduled infusion, I put my local anesthetic on my port area and covered the creamy mess with a strip of Saran wrap to save my clothes from the gooey mess. My mother went with me to this appointment. The nurse took us back to a private room. As we waited for her to return, I looked at my mother's face as she sat across the room from me. She had tears welling up in her eyes. I tried to put on my brave face and tell her everything was going to be okay. Inside I was trembling, not knowing what to expect. It was a bit uncomfortable when the nurse accessed the port, since the area still felt tender. However, truth be told, during all my treatments I was on edge when they would access my port. Sometimes it would be more uncomfortable and sting, while other times it was fine. It may have been different nurses having different techniques, or maybe it had to do with how much numbing cream I used prior to the infusion.

For eight weeks I received AC (Adriamycin and cyclophosphamide). Every two weeks they administered the drug while I sucked on ice chips (to avoid mouth sores.) The first few days after the infusion I would feel nauseous, tired, hot in the face, and have a headache. I hated all the drugs I was taking, so after day four or five I would stop taking all the nausea medications. I would start to feel pretty good after about day 10 or 11, and then it was time to get another dose. I would have to psych myself up on day two to day nine after the infusions to give myself a shot (in the stomach). I hate needles, so to have to do this 28 times was a little challenging. This helped my blood cell count; however, it would also cause aches in my lower back and thighs. Sometimes the pain was so severe that I needed a strong dose of Tylenol.

I opted not to use cooling caps to save my hair. Despite using the caps during the first two rounds, my hair started falling out. It seemed futile. First, my hair isn't very thick to begin with, and second, I didn't want to interfere with the chemo going to my head since breast cancer can metastasize to the brain. After the second round, I noticed my hair coming out in clumps. I would try so hard to lightly wash or brush my hair, but inevitably huge amounts would come out. This was a little traumatic for me, so I told my husband to just shave my head. For me, this was the best decision; it was like ripping off the band-aid. I know it sounds odd, but it was also a bonding moment for me and my husband. I think my hair loss was hardest on my nine-year-old daughter. At times she would just look at me with big sad eyes, not saying a word. However, she and my husband were so good about regularly telling me how beautiful I looked. I was not going to be winning any beauty pageants, but words are powerful. Their sweet compliments gave me confidence to bare my bald head in public.

During my last round of AC, I could not bear the thought of sucking on the ice chips. I know this sounds strange, but by the third round of this drug I was gagging on the ice chips. For my final round of the "red devil" I opted for a very cold Jamba Juice to suck on instead. I don't think I could drink that flavor today though—association is a bizarre thing. This is also when my eyelashes and eyebrows finally went. They had hung on for two months.

For three months, I received Taxol weekly. Personally, it was not as bad as the previous rounds of chemotherapy. The best part was I didn't have to give myself shots anymore. I wasn't nauseous, just tired and with lots of aches and pains. The biggest challenge for me was the "ice therapy." Remember the booties and mittens Rhonda loaned me? I would freeze them before my treatments. Then for the full hour infusion I would have to rotate the frozen booties and mittens. I did not want neuropathy, so I was willing to feel like I had frostbite on my hands and feet for the duration of the infusion. July 9 was my last chemo infusion; 16 rounds of chemo, and I was beginning to sprout hair. Woohoo!

There are some annoying things that you don't realize come with chemo—and people don't tell you about. Losing hair is a bit uncomfortable. My scalp would tingle and feel sensitive to the touch. You lose ALL your hair on your body. This includes your nose hairs. Now this doesn't sound so bad, but when chemo causes you to have a runny drippy nose this is not a good combination. When you bend over, it all just freely drips out your nose. I never thought I would miss boogers and nose hairs. Not only was my nose a faucet, but my eyes would water incessantly. I felt like I needed a Kleenex wrapped around my face. And the gas for me was horrible! After my infusions I would get the hiccups, but worse than that was the flatulence—we don't need to discuss that.

Yes, I felt like garbage most of the time, but I tried to still find the positives. As I previously stated, you lose ALL body hair, so it was great to not have to even think about shaving all those months. Also, I saved time and money on hair and makeup products. There were no expectations placed on my appearance. I didn't want to wear a wig, as they are scratchy, uncomfortable, and hot. I figured if I was going through all this crap, then people could at least be visibly aware, and they may be a little more patient or kind. It was kind of fun to get little kids' reactions too. I had to laugh inside when I could see the parent squirm when their young child would innocently comment or question my appearance. I did find some cute scarfs, so if I felt like dressing up or going to church I would "accessorize" with a scarf on my head. Another bonus to all of this, I had my own personal parking space every time I went for appointments. Parking is always a challenge at this medical facility, but there is an area in the parking lot reserved for infusion patients. Hey, it's those little things in life that we need to appreciate, even if it is just a parking space.

Exactly one month later, I had surgery to remove the tumors and conduct an axillary dissection. My biggest fear was coming out of surgery with severe nerve damage, since one of my tumors was near a major nerve bundle. I remember waking up with excruciating pain radiating down my left arm. Normally after surgeries the nurses find it challenging to wake me up. However, this time was different. As soon as I started waking, I began moaning about a horrible pain down my left arm. My husband told them he didn't want to take me home when I was in such discomfort. We convinced them to admit me and let me stay the night. They gave me some nerve pain medication that seemed to help. I became fearful that this was going to be my new normal, if I did indeed have major nerve damage. My mind became distracted as family members one by one came back to visit me in the recovery room. However, tears started streaming down my face when my 15-year-old daughter came to my bedside with "Fight Song" playing on her phone for me. I was feeling so beat up and discouraged, but she reminded me of my anthem. I still had a lot of fight left in me. The following morning my surgeon came in and told me that she was able to preserve the nerves, and that the pain was likely from the position held during surgery. The pain was more tolerable, and I was starting to focus more on the expander and drains. I was discharged that afternoon.

Two weeks later my drains were removed, and I was able to get another "fill" in my expander. It's also about this time that my eyelashes and eyebrows started making a comeback. The severe discomfort in the armpit area was getting better, but I was still limited with the use of my arms.

Three weeks later (end of September) I received four tattoos required to help align my body for radiation. Definitely not cute tattoos; they look like blackheads. I also had to have my left expander deflated for radiation because having a flatter surface is optimal for radiation. You know it looks bad when your plastic surgeon hands you a mirror and says, "Brace yourself." My left breast looked like a crushed soda can. However, the discomfort of it all took my mind off it. There was horrible soreness, as the expander felt like the perimeters were digging into me. The discomfort began to subside after a few days.

Radiation was every day, Monday through Friday. Twenty-eight rounds of radiation using the "deep breathing" method. Basically, I would have to take a deep breath and hold it before they would "zap" me. This would help alleviate some of the risk to my heart because the cancer was on my left side. I began to develop a rapport with my radiation techs; after all, I saw these two every day for more than a month. I recall having a treatment on Halloween. The entire clinic was dressed in costumes. My techs were hard to take seriously that day. I had a giraffe and a lion giving me instructions. They asked me where my costume was, and I witfully told them that I was the "Uni-boober." I could joke about it, because I knew it was temporary. My skin didn't get really burnt until the last week of radiation, about the 23rd round. My underarm area became severely bright red and raw. Thankfully, I couldn't really feel it because of the numbness due to nerve damage. The redness peaked about four days after the final round of radiation. With lots of ointment and cream the skin looked well healed after two weeks.

Seven months later I was able to have my expander out and get my new implants. The exchange surgery is not a bad recovery. You must limit your arm movement for six weeks. In 2013 I had silicone implants, and this time I went with saline. I prefer the saline. Sorry to say, neither option feels like a natural breast. They are both hard if you ask me. The reason I prefer the saline implants is they are not cold. My breasts were always cold with the silicone. Think about it; you have no breast tissue to help regulate the temperature. I always felt like I had a cool compress on my chest. I don't have that with the saline; they are warm. With saline, I assume my body heat can penetrate the saline better than silicone. I don't have cold compresses anymore!

I have to give thanks to God, our family, church family, and friends. They truly sustained us during this past year and a half. The love and support that was given to us was beyond amazing. There was always someone there to help with housework, meals, kids, and chemo appointments. I feel so blessed to have such an amazing support network; we never felt alone. It seemed like daily we would get a boost from someone, whether it was the above-mentioned acts, a prayer, card, flowers, text, or some other act of service. My husband is a teacher, and he would come home periodically with stacks of handwritten cards from students. I was so touched when he brought home 1,000 Origami cranes that the kids had made me. There is a Japanese tradition, *senbazuru*. It is believed that if one folds 1,000 origami cranes, one's wish will come true. It has also become a symbol of hope and healing during challenging times. The constant love and support we received continually boosted our spirits and gave us enormous strength. We will forever be grateful.

I have recovered from the reconstruction surgery and am doing physical therapy. I have good days and I have better days. There are still residual effects from the surgeries. My range of motion with my left arm is limited. I do have some nerve damage, and there is annoying tightness in my underarm and axillary area. I am hoping that with physical therapy and time things will start to loosen up, and I can get my range of motion back. I have signed up for five more years of hormone therapy. I get a monthly injection of Lupron to suppress the ovaries while I take a daily aromatase inhibitor, anastrozole. The side effects are not fun. Severe joint stiffness and pain with constant hot flashes, to name a couple. But no pity party here because "There is always someone who has it worse."

10

C-SQUARED

Mari's Treatment

With my breast cancer diagnosis came overwhelming uncertainty and stress, along with a whirlwind of medical appointments. I had an appointment with a nurse in the surgery department within a few days of my diagnosis. At the appointment I learned that my tumor was estrogen and progesterone positive (ER+, PR+) and HER2 negative (HER2-). Due to these tumor characteristics and my known positive lymph node, my cancer care team recommended that I undergo surgery as the first step in my treatment plan.

I met with the breast surgeon one week later. She was extremely calm, compassionate, and knowledgeable—everything I needed at that moment. She greeted me with a big hug and assured me she was going to take excellent care of me. She took the time to answer all my and my husband's questions; yes, he had questions too. But most importantly, she communicated very clearly my surgery options, which were either a lumpectomy with a breast reduction or a single mastectomy. I explained to her that my main goal was to be here long-term for my family and that I was not concerned about keeping my breast. She explained that in my case a lumpectomy followed by radiation would be equally effective as a single mastectomy. However, in making my decision, she highly recommended that I consider how anxious I would be about my breast cancer coming back. If removing the entire breast would help me worry less about this possibility, a single mastectomy might be the better option for me. In order to help me make my decision, she wanted me to meet with the plastic surgeon, who could provide me with more details regarding the reconstructive aspect of my surgery.

My appointment with the plastic surgeon did not go as well as I had anticipated. As most plastic surgeons are, he was very focused on the aesthetics of my breasts. But I was certainly not prepared to hear him call my breasts "droopy" and "saggy" over and over again. Being a 42-year -old woman who had breastfed both of my children, I was well aware that my breasts were not as "firm" and "perky" as they once were. However, it would not have been my personal choice to seek breast reconstructive surgery but for my traumatic breast cancer diagnosis. For this reason, I expected a higher level of respect and grace surrounding the discussion of the reconstructive aspect of my surgery. Nonetheless, I sat quietly and listened very carefully to what he had to say. He provided me with very honest and accurate medical advice and was also very knowledgeable when answering my questions. But thanks to this appointment, I learned very early on in my breast cancer journey that not all doctors are innately disposed to be understanding and compassionate.

I spent the next couple of days processing all the information that I had learned from both my breast surgeon and plastic surgeon. I also did a lot of my own research and had many discussions about the pros and cons of both surgical options with my sister and husband, the two people I trusted most to help guide and support me with this life-changing decision. Ultimately, I had to make the decision that was best for me. After very careful consideration and listening to my intuition and the callings of my heart, I decided to proceed with a lumpectomy and breast reduction. To be honest, I second-guessed my decision the moment I made it, but I am certain that I would have second-guessed whatever decision I made that day. I focused on what was important at that moment, which was moving forward with surgery and removing the cancer so that my cancer care team could have more information to help them decide on the next steps of my treatment plan.

After deciding how to move forward with surgery and

as the initial shock of my breast cancer diagnosis subsided, I immediately thought of my children and how to tell them I had breast cancer. I was more worried about them than I was about myself at that point. And I could not help but feel guilty about the difficult journey we were about to embark on as a family due to my diagnosis. I spent years in therapy working on healing from the trauma of my husband's thyroid cancer diagnoses, so I had a very trusted therapist to help me with these feelings. How to deliver the news to my children, who were six and 11 years old at the time of my diagnosis, in an age-appropriate manner was the focus of many therapy sessions. Each family has to find its own unique way of communicating, and for mine, it was waiting until we had more information about the cancer and its treatment. We quickly realized that no matter how young our children were, it was important for them to know about my diagnosis. We did not want them learning of my diagnosis from others or by overhearing a conversation. I also wanted to assure my children that I was there for them, despite having breast cancer, and that they could always bring their fears and questions to me or their father. My husband and I discussed my diagnosis with each of our children separately. We did not want to overwhelm them with information, so we told them just enough to understand what was going on. To my surprise, they handled the initial news of my diagnosis very well. My older son only asked my husband if I was going to be okay. It was a huge load off my mind to share this news with them and see that it did not bother them, which gave me a bit of peace and allowed me to focus on my upcoming surgery.

Before I knew it, it was already the night before my surgery. I was scheduled for a lumpectomy with a breast reduction and an axillary dissection to remove my lymph nodes. I had never had any kind of surgery before, so the nerves had set in. However, I was overwhelmed by the outpouring of love and support from family and close friends, and I could hardly keep up with all the phone calls and texts I was receiving. I hardly slept that night, but I woke up feeling ready to take on the next step in my breast cancer journey. Once at the hospital, preparation for surgery took some time. I met with the anesthesiologist, breast surgeon, and plastic surgeon, among others. I also got a visit from a breast cancer peer navigator. My healthcare provider has a peer support program that connects newly diagnosed patients with survivors to help navigate their journey. The first step in this program is to meet with the patient on the day of surgery. The peer navigator spoke to my husband and me and told us a little bit about her journey with breast cancer. Her story of survivorship and beating cancer four times was very inspiring and well-timed. Most importantly, she provided me with some great advice that I carry with me to this day. She told me that breast cancer is a journey that must be taken moment by moment, sometimes breath by breath, other times step by step. My husband kissed me goodbye, told me he loved me, and that he would be there when I woke up. I took the words of the navigator and my husband with me as tears streamed down my cheeks while being rolled into the frigid operating room. The lights were glaring in my face and I was surrounded by a team of medical staff. I have a faint memory of being asked to declare what procedure I was having done as my eyes slowly closed and I drifted off to sleep.

After what felt like a short nap, I opened my eyes and asked the nurse checking on my vitals if she knew when I was going into surgery. She looked at me and said, "Oh honey, you are in postoperative recovery. Your surgery is all done!" I was shocked and relieved to hear this information. I realized I had thick bandages wrapped so tightly around my chest that I could barely move, and a drain sticking out of the side of the bandages filling up with blood. And as promised, my husband was sitting right beside me. He had already spoken to the breast surgeon and shared with me that at least two more positive lymph nodes were discovered during surgery. We would not have the full pathology report for another week or so, but this was not the news I wanted to hear. My time in postoperative recovery was very short as the anesthesia wore off quickly and the pain was manageable, so I was discharged.

The week following my surgery was uneventful. I forced myself to rest and give my body time to heal. I also took daily walks, which became my steadfast ritual to get my body moving, get some fresh air into my lungs, and clear my mind of stress. The bandages wrapped so tightly around my breasts were extremely uncomfortable and itchy, and I thought I was ready to have them removed. But as the day of my postoperative appointment neared, I became increasingly anxious about seeing the appearance of my new breast and getting my pathology report. My first post-operative appointment was with the plastic surgeon. He removed the bandages and drain, and I cried hysterically the entire time. To a doctor, a scar is a normal process for healing skin. But to me, the scars were a constant reminder of the pain and suffering I was enduring, and it was too much for me to bear. My doctor was pleased with the results of the surgery and how everything was healing, so he encouraged me to look at my new breast in the mirror in his office. I politely declined and told him I was not ready to do so yet. Contrary to my last appointment with him, he was very compassionate and understanding, and he did not force me to do anything I was not ready for. I was also scheduled to meet with my breast surgeon next to discuss my pathology report. I had mentally prepared myself for bad news, and my stomach was in knots as I waited in the examination room. I was hoping she would have information that would put my mind at ease, but that was not the case. Unfortunately, my pathology report was not ready. So I left her office with the same uncertainty as when I arrived, still not knowing exactly what I was facing.

It did not take long for my pathology report to be ready after my appointments. Within a couple of days, I received a call from my breast surgeon. My husband took the call, as I did not feel strong enough to hear the news directly. She told him that she had both good and bad news. She started with the good news, that my margins were clear. However, the bad news was really bad. The cancer had spread to 11 of the 16 lymph nodes that were removed! Even though I had mentally prepared myself, I was still stunned and scared to have so many positive lymph nodes. Due to the high number of positive lymph nodes, the probability of the cancer having spread to other parts of my body was higher, so the breast surgeon wanted me to have a PET scan before determining the next step in my treatment plan. The breast surgeon ended the call with some words of encouragement, telling my husband that she felt confident that she had removed it all.

My PET scan was scheduled for the following week. Upon my arrival, the technician explained the procedure and answered my questions. I received an intravenous injection of a tracer dose of radioactive material. The level of radioactivity is very low and thankfully has no side effects. Then I had to wait for about an hour before the PET scan could begin. The PET scan itself was quick and took only about 15 minutes. I was relieved when it was over, and ready to be reunited with my husband, who was waiting for me in the waiting room. The technician informed me on my way out that the results should not take more than a few days. I found myself suffering from severe "scanxiety" in the days surrounding my PET scan. Scanxiety is a term often used to describe the anxious feelings that arise in the time leading up to a cancer imagining scan, during the scan, and while waiting for results. I waited 10 long and agonizing days for the results of my PET scan. I kept thinking about what the technician had told me on my way out, that the results should take only a couple of days. I was convinced that the cancer had spread to every part of my body where I felt daily aches and pains. I should have been a better advocate for myself and called my breast surgeon to check on the status of my PET scan results. But I was too scared to know the results, so I did not. When she finally called with the results, it was again not the news I wanted to hear. Although there were no signs of the cancer spreading to the parts of my body where breast cancer usually spreads, there were more active than normal cells in my right ovary and I had nodules on my thyroid. On the one hand I was relieved, but on the other hand I was now terrified that I had ovarian and thyroid cancer too. Additional imaging of my ovaries and thyroid was scheduled right away.

In the meantime, I received a call from an oncology nurse navigator. My newly assigned oncologist asked her to call me and initiate the process for starting chemotherapy. My family was planning to travel to Hawaii with two other families, our closest friends, in just a couple of weeks. This was something we had been doing every year in November for three years, and my family was really looking forward to this trip. I asked the oncology nurse navigator if she thought it would be advisable for me to make this trip with my family before starting chemotherapy. She said she would check with my oncologist and get back to me. While I waited for the oncology nurse navigator to get back to me, I went to my appointments for a transvaginal ultrasound and a thyroid ultrasound to rule out cancer in those parts of my body. I also decided to have blood drawn for genetic testing because of my mother's history of breast cancer.

It was a Wednesday afternoon and the day before Halloween. I had just returned home after having my thyroid ultrasound done when my phone rang. It was the oncology nurse navigator with more discouraging news. She informed me that my oncologist wanted me to start chemotherapy right away and was recommending that I not travel to Hawaii. So she scheduled an appointment with the oncologist the following Tuesday. I was very sad to hear that I could not travel to Hawaii, but doing what was best for my health was the most important thing. I wanted to ensure that I was around for future trips with my family, so I did not hesitate to follow my oncologist's orders. However, I encouraged my husband to make the trip with our children without me. It would be a good distraction for all of them after the stressful and difficult months we'd endured. He refused to even entertain this option and said we would either all go or none of us would go. In a way I was relieved to hear this, because I was anxiously waiting for the results of my ultrasounds and genetic testing. It was Halloween, one of my family's favorite holidays, and I was determined to make the day fun despite being distracted and overwhelmed by everything going on. And to make matters worse, I received a voicemail from my OB-GYN right before heading out to a Halloween celebration and trick or treating. She did not leave any details in her message other than that she would try reaching me the next day. Even though she did not provide me with any details, I knew the call had something to do with my transvaginal ultrasound. And I could not help but think the worst.

Halloween night was a blur. I was physically present for the festivities and went trick or treating with my children, but my mind was elsewhere. When I woke up the next morning, all I could think about was the telephone call I was going to have that day with my OB-GYN. My children had the day off from school and were home with me all day, but they were left to their own devices and ate Halloween candy for breakfast, chips for lunch, and played video games nonstop. Not my finest parenting moments, but I was paralyzed by fear and anxiety and did not have the strength to do for them the things I normally did, like feed and entertain them. It was late afternoon when I finally received a call from my OB-GYN. It was not the news I was expecting to hear, but I felt a huge sense of relief when she informed me that the probability of the cysts found on my ovaries being cancerous was low. With that said, however, she wanted me to have a CA 125 blood test, a test used to measure levels of a tumor marker associated with ovarian cancer. She said it would take a few days to get the results and then she would confer with OB oncology. As soon as my husband returned home from work that evening, I went to the lab and had my blood drawn.

The telephone call with my OB-GYN lifted some weight off my shoulders and gave me a renewed sense of hope. She called me on Monday morning with the results of my CA 125 blood test, which was normal, and had also discussed my ultrasound and blood test results with OB oncology. They were all in agreement that the probability of the cysts on my ovaries being cancerous was low and just wanted me to have a follow-up ultrasound in six months. My OB-GYN also informed me about the results of my thyroid ultrasound, even though this was outside her area of expertise. She was surprised that I had not received a call about the results and could sense that waiting for them was extremely anxiety-inducing for me. She read the results and said everything looked normal and no follow-up was necessary. I shed tears of joy and let my OB-GYN know that I was so grateful for her diligent attention to my care. Along the way I also received a call about the results of my genetic testing, and I had no mutations on any of the genes associated with an increased risk of cancer. Waiting for medical test results proved to be one of the hardest parts of my journey; staying calm like everyone encouraged me to do was much easier said than done.

The very next morning was my first oncology appointment. There had been so much panic around the unknown in the months leading up to this appointment. Although I was extremely nervous, I felt ready to move forward with a treatment plan. When the oncologist walked in, she firmly shook my husband's hand and gave me a warm hug. She asked how I was doing, and although I said, "Fine," I am sure the look on my face told her otherwise. Before discussing my medical condition, she shared a personal story of hope about her mother having cancer and the reason she became an oncologist. Little by little I felt a sense of calm come over me. As my body language changed and became more relaxed, she went on to discuss my diagnosis, invasive ductal carcinoma, stage 3a. The pain of hearing those words is something that will stay with me for the rest of my life. However, having ruled out cancer in my ovaries and thyroid, the oncologist said I was on the "good train" now, and she wanted me to stay on it. That meant months of chemotherapy followed by radiation and daily hormone therapy. Before all of that was set to begin, she reversed course on her previous recommendation not to travel to Hawaii and gave me the green light to go. Although this was good news, I left the appointment having mixed emotions, both happy about being able to go, but worried about delaying my treatment, even if only by a couple of days.

I spent the next week getting ready for my first chemotherapy treatment, which was scheduled for the morning after my return from Hawaii. There was blood work, a MUGU scan (a test using a radioactive tracer and a special camera that assesses the function of the heart), a port placement, an appointment with the oncology nurses about my chemotherapy medications, and a chemotherapy orientation class. It was the night before our flight and I was exhausted, both physically and emotionally. We were going for only five days so there was very little to pack, but I barely had the energy to do it. Our flight was very early the next morning, and I just was not feeling the same excitement about this trip as I had felt in years past.

We stayed at our favorite resort in Oahu, one very familiar to us, as this was our fourth year in a row going in November. It felt like home the second we arrived. The kids wanted to do all their favorite things, such as snorkeling in the ocean, eating shaved ice, floating on the lazy river, and going down the water slides. Our room had a beautiful ocean view, where we watched the sun rise and set almost every day. We also took daily walks on the beach. The sound of the waves crashing on the beach was music to my ears. But the best part about this trip was doing all these things with our best friends.

We shared so many laughs and good times, which brought some much-needed normalcy into my life. Although I had been hesitant to take this trip because of the uncertainty of my health, it was the best medicine and just the respite I needed before starting chemotherapy.

My first chemotherapy treatment was the morning after returning home from our trip. The chemotherapy portion of my treatment plan consisted of two phases. The first phase was a combination of Adriamycin and cyclophosphamide (AC), which was administered every other week for four cycles. Adriamycin is often called the "red devil," both for its bright red color and its nasty side effects. My husband called it Pinot Noir due to its color and my love for wine. The second phase was Taxol, which was administered every week for 12 weeks. A close family member, usually my husband, accompanied me to each treatment, where we were always greeted with a smile by the kindest and most compassionate staff in the infusion center. When my husband could not be there due to a work commitment, he always made sure to have someone else lined up, like my cousin or nephew. I always appreciated having someone there, but my husband was the most calming presence and always knew what to do or say to make me feel better. He talked to me when I needed someone to talk to, or just sat quietly and held my hand when I did not have the energy to talk. And he always helped me put on my cooling mittens and slippers I wore to prevent neuropathy during my Taxol treatments. I also had frequent visits from the peer navigator who I met at my surgery. It was always nice to catch up with her and hear her stories of hope and survival.

I suffered from several of the typical side effects from the AC treatments. I developed a metallic taste in my mouth and had mouth sores. I could not tolerate any perfume or candle fragrance and disliked foods and drinks I once loved. Things just did not smell or taste the same anymore. I also had mild nausea, severe heartburn, frequent headaches, and extreme fatigue. But the most traumatic side effect of all was losing the hair on my body, from my head to my toes. The hair on my scalp began falling out about ten days after my first AC treatment. It started with a tingling sensation on my scalp, and with each day that passed, more and more hair fell out. The trauma from watching my hair fall out became so severe that I made the decision to shave my head. I had my husband do it one morning after he dropped the kids off at school. I cried as he shaved off more and more hair, but he maintained his composure the entire time and hugged me tightly when he was done. He also stood beside me when I glimpsed my bald head in the mirror for the first time and took my despair and frustration out on my sink top. Into the trash went my beloved collection of styling creams, brushes, and sprays, but most importantly, my hair. My husband told me that I had a perfect shaped head, not exactly a compliment I was looking for, but sometimes humor is a good medicine! Hair loss is extremely personal, and there is no right or wrong way to cope with it. I never left the house without a wig or a hat, though I envied the strength of women I saw rocking their bald and beautiful heads.

I also suffered from a less common side effect about halfway through my chemotherapy treatments. After arriving at the infusion center for my treatment and having my vitals taken, which is standard care before each treatment, my heart rate and blood pressure were both dangerously high. I figured it was just my nerves getting the best of me, as they often did. The oncology nurse was not concerned at first and assumed my blood pressure and heart rate would be better when she rechecked them, but they were not. In fact, they were getting worse. After an hour with no improvement, she decided to send a message to my oncologist while I tried to relax and take deep breaths. She also ordered an electrocardiogram (EKG) to measure the electrical signals in my heart. The EKG was administered in the infusion center and the electrical signals in my heart were normal, but my heart rate was still dangerously high. Shortly after completing the EKG, my oncologist called and ordered a CT scan of my upper body to rule out a pulmonary embolism. A pulmonary embolism is a condition in which one or more arteries in the lungs is blocked by a blood clot. I felt scared and just wanted to have my treatment. After having the CT scan my oncologist felt it was safe to proceed with my treatment. Although I did not have the results of my CT scan, I was allowed to go home after finishing my treatment. But just a few minutes after arriving at home, my phone rang, and it was my oncologist. The CT scan confirmed I had a pulmonary embolism, and she recommended I immediately start blood thinning medication to dissolve the clot. She explained the pulmonary embolism was caused by the chemotherapy drugs, and that I was at high risk for developing another embolism. I returned to the infusion center and an oncology nurse gave me an injection of blood thinning medication. I was required to take blood thinning medications in pill form until three months after completing treatment. Although it was an extremely overwhelming and stressful day, I was thankful the embolism was discovered before anything more serious occurred, and my cousin was there to support me, as I surely needed him.

Then, the entire world changed. With four Taxol treatments left, on March 11, 2020, a global pandemic was declared due to the novel coronavirus (COVID-19). COVID-19 is a very contagious respiratory and vascular disease that was first identified in Wuhan, China, and quickly spread to the rest of the world. People with a weakened immune system, such as those undergoing chemotherapy treatment, are more likely to experience dangerous symptoms if infected with COVID-19. On March 19, 2020, the governor of California issued a stay-at-home order to protect the health and well-being of all

Californians and to establish consistency across the state in order to slow the spread of COVID-19. Schools were closed, and my children began distance learning. My husband also began working from home. We left our house only for essential reasons, like medical appointments, and ordered all our groceries online and had them delivered. Toilet paper and Clorox wipes were hot items. When we were outside of our home, we maintained a social distance from others and wore face masks. I was one of those people all the social distancing measures were helping to protect, and part of the "cure" that must not be worse than the "problem." Medical care changed too, including mine.

Cancer is hard enough without a pandemic. My healthcare provider took extreme measures to prevent the spread of COVID-19. What were usually in-person appointments became telephone or video appointments. The exception was my chemotherapy treatments. When I went to my chemotherapy treatments, I was required to wear a facemask and was screened for COVID-19 symptoms before entering the facility. Visitors were no longer allowed, so my treatments went from being accompanied by my husband or family to being alone. I was no longer greeted with smiles by the infusion center staff as they were hidden under facemasks and face shields. I felt very isolated, but the infusion center staff stepped in as best as they could. I knew many of them personally after five months of treatment, and they were the backbone I needed during those difficult final treatments. My last treatment was on April 2, 2020. My chemotherapy treatment had a cumulative impact on my physical and mental strength. My husband was so glad that this was the last time he was going to drop me off by myself. I received many well wishes from the infusion center staff as I completed my treatment and a big hug from my husband and children, who greeted me outside when I was done. That evening, my husband gave me the biggest surprise. He wanted to have friends and extended family at our home to greet me after completing my chemotherapy treatment, but that was not an option because of the pandemic. So, using technology, he put a slideshow together that had photos and well wishes recorded from family and friends from all over the globe. The reality of the moment hit me hard; I smiled, cried, and laughed as my family enjoyed the slideshow together.

The next phase of my treatment plan, radiation, started a month and a half after I finished chemotherapy. For my treatment plan, five areas were radiated, and I had sessions five days a week for six weeks, for a total of 30 sessions. The pandemic was still going strong, and the same precautionary measures were in place as with my chemotherapy treatment. No visitors were allowed, so I drove myself to each appointment and was required to wear a face mask. For each session, a machine was used to aim high-energy rays from outside the body into the five areas. I was required to stay extremely still as I lay in the machine. I kept my eyes closed the entire time and listened to the cheerful music that was always playing. After every session I applied moisturizing ointment to the radiated skin before going home. I also made sure to apply additional moisturizing ointment throughout the day to keep the skin hydrated. My skin held up well until the last day, when it finally appeared sunburned and felt itchy. I continued to apply moisturizing ointment after completing radiation, and the skin healed within a couple of weeks. Another side effect I suffered from after a few weeks of radiation was fatigue. I lacked energy for day-to-day activities and took frequent naps. This persisted for several months after completing radiation, but I eventually got my energy back. On my final day of radiation my dear friends waited for me in the parking lot and surprised me with cheers, a banner, balloons, flowers, and champagne. I felt so loved and supported, and will never forget this special day—celebrated at a safe distance.

About the same time I started radiation, I started the hormone therapy phase of my treatment plan. This therapy was recommended because my tumor was estrogen and progesterone positive. The purpose of hormone therapy is to suppress the production of estrogen and progesterone to reduce the risk that cancer will return. I receive a Lupron shot every month in the infusion center where I went for my chemotherapy treatments. The Lupron shot stops the production of these hormones in my ovaries. I was also prescribed anastrozole, a pill which I take daily to stop the production of these hormones by my pituitary gland. The drawback of this therapy is that it causes a premenopausal woman to enter menopause early. The menopause side effects I would begin to experience were hot flashes; joint pain in my neck, hands, elbows, and knees; and stiffness, especially when I first wake up or sit for long periods of time. To alleviate my hot flashes during the night, which prevented me from getting a good night's sleep, I purchased cooling bed sheets. I also take daily walks to keep my joints working better to relieve some of my joint pain.

The last phase of my active treatment plan was reconstructive surgery of my right breast. I needed to have a reduction and lift in order to reclaim breast symmetry. I had a consultation with the same plastic surgeon who performed the reconstructive aspect of my initial breast surgery. I had some reservations about meeting with him again after being subjected to his poor bedside manners the first time. But to my surprise, my experience this time was extremely pleasant, and empathy-filled. He was kind and compassionate and not once did he refer to my breast as "droopy" or "saggy." As COVID-19 restrictions were still in place, I could not have anybody accompany me to surgery, so my husband dropped me off. I was extremely nervous to do this alone, but surgery went very well. I was in and out in about four hours, and I surprisingly had no pain whatsoever. However, the surgery triggered some emotional trauma and I felt as though I were reliving the time between my initial surgery and getting my pathology results—a time that was one of the most difficult weeks of my life. This procedure marked the end of my surgical treatments, but the emotional struggle is something I will continue to work on for some time.

PART IV
INTERVIEWS

She is a beautiful piece of broken pottery,
put back together by her own hands.
And a critical world judges her cracks
while missing the beauty of how
she made herself whole again.

Jm Storm

11

STRONG SURVIVORS

Interviews with Our Mothers

Interview with Rhonda's Mother, Jane Corbett

How long ago was your breast cancer treatment, and how old were you?

I was diagnosed in February 2010. I was 71 years old.

What was your diagnosis?

Triple negative breast cancer, Stage 1. No nodes involved.

What was your treatment?

I had a lumpectomy in February 2010. In March, I had TC (Taxotere and Cytoxan). I had four cycles, once every three weeks. I had a complication after my first chemo. My neutrophils were very low, and my temperature was elevated. I was admitted to the hospital for a few days. Afterwards, I had radiation for 16 sessions, fewer sessions than I had expected.

What worried you the most during this experience?

When I found out that I had triple negative, which is the most aggressive kind of breast cancer, I was very scared that it would metastasize. I asked my oncologist if he would order a CA 15-3 blood test, which is elevated in people with metastatic cancer. The results created a great deal of anxiety for me. Although it was elevated for several months, it eventually returned to normal. I think it may have been elevated due to my skin cancer.

What helped you cope?

I have always kept journals. I dedicated a notebook specifically to cancer and wrote in it every day. Also, my daughter and son-in-law were very attentive. My sister visited from Kentucky as well. My friends drove me to radiation. I went on walks almost every day. My tap group and former coworkers sent gifts.

What was it like to have your daughter in treatment?

I was very shocked when you were diagnosed at such a young age. I felt very guilty that you did not get a mammogram, even though standard practice is not to start until age 40. When you wanted to go to Mexico, I was hesitant to go but am glad that we did, because it created wonderful memories. When you found out you had the VUS on the BRCA-2 and I did too, that also made me feel guilty. What if I had passed that on to you? But you had another type of breast cancer than I did.

What is different about your breast cancer experience than mine?

First, you had it when you were so young. Second, you had estrogen progesterone positive and I had triple negative. Third, you had much more surgery than I did. Fourth, you are taking hormone therapy for estrogen progesterone positive.

What was it like for your grandchildren?

When I had my breast cancer, your daughter was not yet born. She was born only two weeks after I finished radiation. I was afraid that I would not have enough energy to take care of your son, but I did.

How has your life changed after cancer?

I made a list of 22 things that I gave up. Some of them included coffee and wine. I lost all my hair. I had very little appetite. I had very little energy. I never took baths, only showers, because I was afraid of getting an infection. I lost my peace of mind about my health. I couldn't take trips during that time. I couldn't write the next edition of my book. I missed my tap dance recital. I couldn't volunteer. But I also gained a lot. I connected with many friends. I enjoyed armchair travel. When my hair grew back, I let it stay grey. I found a co-author to help me with the next edition of my book. I started volunteering for Breast Cancer Action.

What advice would you give to other survivors?

Take really good care of yourself. Use many resources to help you. Realize that each day is a blessing and live it to the fullest. Help other people who have breast cancer. Finally, sign up for research studies to help contribute to what can be discovered about breast cancer. I participate in Pathways, a study of the quality of life of breast cancer survivors.

Interview with Jennifer's Mother, Faye Amos

How long ago was your breast cancer treatment, and how old were you?

Seven years ago, in 2013. I was 74 years old.

What was your diagnosis?

Estrogen positive invasive ductal carcinoma, Stage 1. No nodes involved.

What was your treatment?

A lumpectomy.

What worried you the most during this experience?

Probably not knowing initially if I was going to have to do chemo or a mastectomy. After meeting with doctors and doing the lumpectomy, I had confidence in the situation. There's different anxiety when you're old and you don't have kids at home. You can't compare a young mother's situation with someone who is 74 and has lived most of their life.

What was it like to have your daughter go through breast cancer treatment?

It was life-altering for me. It created a lot of anxiety and concern for me because you were so young and had young children. If I could have made a deal with God to have Him take me in your place, I would have. It was frightening and it still is frightening.

What helped you cope?
My faith helped me cope; the eternal perspective that I have. I also had good doctors and I put my trust in them and what they were telling me.

How has your life changed after cancer?
It makes you more aware of what a devastating diagnosis it is. I can't say that it's really changed my life. Your diagnosis affected me more than my own.

Interview with Mari's Mother, Juana Perez

How long ago was your breast cancer treatment, and how old were you?

I was diagnosed in 2002, when I was 56 years old.

What was your diagnosis?

In-situ ductal carcinoma, estrogen and progesterone positive, Stage 1. No nodes involved.

What was your treatment?

I had a single side mastectomy in 2002. I later had reconstructive surgery.

What worried you the most during this experience?

I was very scared. My English language is very limited, so I was frightened that I did not understand things. I was worried about leaving behind a husband, children, and grandchildren.

What helped you cope?

I speak with my family every day; I did then too. My daughters gave me strength with positive encouragement and support.

What was it like to have your daughter in treatment?

I was very scared for you. Your children were very young. I couldn't imagine them living without their mother. I would make meals each week and do all I could to support you.

What is different about your breast cancer experience than mine?

I was very uninformed. I only knew that I had breast cancer. I did not have to do chemotherapy or radiation treatments, so seeing my daughter go through that was difficult.

What was it like for your grandchildren?

When I had my breast cancer, two of my grandchildren lived in Spain and two were not yet born. We shielded the grandchildren from what I went through because they were young and far away. Now, one of those grandchildren is a surgeon and the other a nurse in Spain. They help me understand so much now.

How has your life changed after having breast cancer?

I accepted that I had this disease and have been determined to live my life. I do have daily grief believing that I may have passed genes to my daughters related to cancer.

What are some lessons learned from this experience?

Get mammograms regularly and if you have dense breast tissue, ask the medical providers if there are alternate tests.

What advice would you give to other survivors?

Take everything one day at a time Do not be afraid to ask for and accept help from those who care about you. Be grateful for your life. I thank God I am living and able to be a survivor.

12

IN SICKNESS AND IN HEALTH

Interviews with Our Spouses

INTERVIEWS

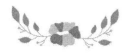

Interview with Rhonda's Spouse, Jorge Eyzaguirre

What are some ways you helped me during treatment?
I went to almost every appointment with you for emotional support. I helped as a nurse and took care of your drains after the surgery. I helped you with the cool caps for chemo. I went to get dry ice and prepped the cool caps in the cooler the night before. I drove you to every chemo and tried to keep you comfortable. I helped with the timer to swap the cool caps. I took care of the kids and gave you space to rest. I did most of the cooking. I would also give you massages to help you sleep and relieve your aches and pains.

What worried you the most during the experience?
The whole idea of cancer is difficult. This was my first time dealing directly with cancer. I was worried that you would not tolerate the treatments. I wondered how you would respond to the treatments. The best way I could handle everything was to focus on one step at a time.

What was it like having me go through treatment?
I was worried throughout the process. It was hard to see you going through that. It also made me concerned about our family's future. I worried about how it would affect our kids.

What was it like for our children?

We tried to keep our kids informed, but not give them unnecessary details. They were young enough to not notice your side effects too much. They still did fine in school. Their teachers were aware of the situation. The kids wanted to hang out with you more than they could, and missed being with you. I think they handled it well and maintained their innocence because of their ages.

What helped you cope?

I tried to keep busy. I got things done to keep my mind from going down a dark path. I took it one day at a time. I focused on your comfort level. I didn't want to show much emotion around you so you wouldn't have more to worry about. We have learned to make health a priority. We are focusing on healthy eating and exercising more, but cancer is always in the back of our minds.

What advice would you give to other caregivers?

Cancer affects everyone; it affects the whole family. It affects the kids and the spouse. You have to take care of yourself too. Pick up a hobby or some activity to help your mental health. It's going to be difficult for a while, but you'll get through it.

Interview with Jennifer's Spouse, Jeff Dresser

What are some ways you helped me during treatment?
I attended some of your chemo infusions to help with the ice treatments, rotating the frozen booties and gloves. I took on more household responsibilities. I made sure my family attended church each Sunday even when you couldn't go. I also tried to maintain a positive attitude.

What worried you the most during the experience?
The scariest moments were waiting for test results like PET scans to see how far it had spread. I was so worried I would be left alone as a single father to raise four small children. I also worried about you having negative reactions to chemo or radiation.

What helped you cope?
We would have a couple's prayer together before each of your infusions; prayer that your vital organs wouldn't be damaged, and that the chemo would work. I tried to maintain a normal schedule as much as possible. Going to work was good because it took my mind off things. Your positive attitude and outlook helped me be positive. Love and support from family, friends, co-workers and students was a huge strength.

How has your marriage changed since I had breast cancer?

It has brought us closer together. We don't bicker about minor issues and we appreciate every day together more. We don't take anything for granted; nothing is a guarantee in life. You have a vision of what your future is supposed to look like, but this opens your eyes and makes you appreciate your time now because tomorrow is not guaranteed.

What advice would you give to other caregivers of spouses with breast cancer?

Make yourself available. Have a positive mindset and be encouraging. Find time for yourself—time for walks, time to ponder and reflect. Lean on family and friends for support and express gratitude to those who step up in times of need.

Interview with Mari's Spouse, Elias Guzman

How did you find out about my breast cancer?

It was our anniversary. I was at work and we had planned a nice dinner at a great restaurant on the river. I immediately sensed hesitation in your voice. You were concerned about a lump you found in your left breast on your commute into work. You were looking for reassurance from me that "it" was nothing. While I gave you the reassurance you needed, I was privately concerned. Your mother had breast cancer. I had thyroid cancer. I thought, there is no way that now you could have cancer. So, while I aligned with your feelings of "it's probably nothing," I felt the fog of my inevitable concern slowly roll in. I provided you with all the comfort and reassurance that I could. I do not think we went to dinner that night. But, from that day our lives have forever changed.

What worried you the most during the experience?

I was most worried about you. I quickly saw that our children were fine because they did not grasp the gravity of what was occurring. But cancer was a wrecking ball. With each strike it took a piece of you, blow by blow. But I think you surprised yourself by your great strength and determination. While this disease will continue to be a dark cloud in your life, each day the sun will be a little brighter and, as the days, months, and years pass, the memories of the dark clouds will be a distant memory of your past. I was also concerned for our children. Unlike my own journey, I knew that this time our children would see a sick parent. A bald parent. But, to my surprise, our children did not appear to be affected very much by your journey. Most of that was due to your sheer strength and courage to fight this disease while continuing to be the fantastic mother you are. I tried to fill our home each day with optimism and hope. I answered your daily questions of concern with positivity. You needed reassurance.

What helped you cope?

We made the decision to try, as best as we could, to keep things normal for our children. So, I stayed busy shuttling our children around town almost each day with all their activities. I was in awe at your strength, even at times when I know you had none (i.e., Thanksgiving and Christmas during chemo). We also leaned on our friends, too. Our wonderful friends congregated with us, which helped us escape into normalcy when we needed it most—BBQs, swimming, music. I tried to stay busy by doing things around our home; perhaps sometimes in a robotic manner. We watched USC football games together (on television), which is our family tradition each year.

What advice would you give to other caregivers of spouses with breast cancer?

The role of the caregiver is important. If you were the assistant coach, you will now be the interim head coach. If you were the head coach, you would not have your assistant coach. The point is that your life will change. But, by remembering that your daily struggle is an investment in a more hopeful and healthy tomorrow, you will get through it. Do your best to be with your spouse through this journey. Sometimes it is your quirky ways and mannerisms that will remind your spouse of normalcy because it is you being you. Being there also lets your spouse know they are not alone. Just be you. Give your spouse your time.

13

RESILIENCE ACROSS THE AGES

Interviews with Our Children

Interview with Rhonda's Daughter
Age 10 (6 at diagnosis)

How did you find out about my cancer?
You and Dad told us.

What do you remember about my cancer?
You started to lose your hair. You bought a wig [a hair topper]. Nana visited a lot. Dad went to chemotherapy with you. You didn't do much at home. You stayed in your bed mostly. You would come down to eat.

What was the hardest part for you of my cancer?
Probably you not interacting with us as much. You did less of everything. You didn't go out that much. Dad made most of the dinners. We didn't play many games with you.

How was your teacher involved?
My teacher would ask me how I was doing sometimes, and how my mom was doing.

What did you tell your peers?
I remember telling them my mom had cancer. They felt sorry for me. Some people told me that their moms had cancer too.

What helped you cope?

I didn't really know what it was, so I wasn't that scared. I drew a lot. I played with Marshmallow [pet rabbit]. I went to Camp Kesem. We did chats at the end of the night before we went to sleep. There were different questions every night, about who had it [cancer], what kind, ways to cope.

What advice would you give to other kids whose parents have cancer?

I would say that my mom had cancer too, and she is okay now.

Interview with Rhonda's Son
Age 13 (9 at diagnosis)

How did you find out about my cancer?

You and Dad told me. I remember coming home one day and you gave me a book. My sister got a different book. My book was about a boy whose mother had breast cancer. I asked you why you gave the book to me, and you said you found out you had breast cancer.

What do you remember about my cancer?

I remember I didn't tell anyone until the end. I remember picking you up from the doctor's sometimes. I remember seeing you talk on the phone a lot. Even during the first time I went to Camp Kesem, I was quiet and didn't really say much.

What was the hardest part for you of my cancer?

The hardest part was seeing you come back from the chemo. I remember before cancer you were very energetic. During cancer it seemed like you swapped with someone else. Because you were drowsy. Your senses were heightened. During chemo you would say from your bedroom the exact ingredients we were using in the kitchen.

How was your teacher involved?

She wasn't that involved. I didn't want to talk with her about it. As I said before, I kept a lot of stuff to myself. I felt like it wasn't exactly something I wanted to share.

What did you tell your peers?

I didn't tell most of my friends anything. I just told two close friends that my mom had breast cancer. They listened to me and said they were sorry.

What helped you cope?

I liked reading comics. I would play videogames or soccer. I talked to my sister. Camp Kesem was fun because everyone there had also gone through it and knew what it was like.

What advice would you give to other kids whose parents have cancer?

It is good to talk to people. Camp Kesem is something that can really help. Don't make it get you down on your attitude. Most cancers aren't that deadly, from what I know. If you have a pet, it is fun to play with your pet.

Interview with Jennifer's Younger Daughter
Age 11 (9 at second diagnosis)

What was the hardest part for you of my cancer?

Seeing you struggle; like when you were in your hospital bed after surgery. Also, watching Dad shave your head and seeing you bald for months.

What helped you cope?

That I had my Heavenly Father comforting me. When I would pray it felt like He was telling me not to worry because everything was going to be okay. You would tell me everything was going to be okay. Also, staying busy with gymnastics and playing with friends would keep my mind off it.

What advice would you give to other kids whose parents have cancer?

To pray and to help as much as you can.

Interview with Jennifer's Older Daughter
Age 16 (14 at second diagnosis)

What was the hardest part for you of my cancer?

Watching you go through it. Seeing you in your hospital bed

looking weak with drains and a bald head. It affected my moods. I felt like you couldn't be there for me as much, because you were often gone to appointments, recovering or sleeping.

What helped you cope?
The support from friends and family. Listening to music and praying.

What advice would you give to other kids whose parents have cancer?
Try to help members of your family with stuff and being there for each other, because you are all going through it together.

Interview with Jennifer's Younger Son
Age 19 (17 at second diagnosis)

What was the hardest part for you of my cancer?
Having the fear of losing you. Also, seeing the pain you were going through like when you were weak and bald from chemo.

What helped you cope?
Having faith that you would get better. Also staying busy and keeping my mind off it.

What advice would you give to other kids whose parents have cancer?
Be as helpful as possible. Stay positive and stay busy.

Interview with Jennifer's Older Son
Age 22 (20 at second diagnosis)

How did you find out about my cancer?
You called me when I was away at college. I was on campus and went into a private room. After I got off the phone, I broke down crying.

What was the hardest part for you of my cancer?
The fear of not knowing. It was back again, and I didn't know how bad it was going to be. I feared you were going to die.

What helped you cope?
Talking to friends and family about it. Prayer.

What advice would you give to other kids whose parents have cancer?
Have hope. Be supportive. Seek out a strong support system.

Interview with Mari's Younger Son
Age 7 (6 at diagnosis)

How did you find out about my cancer?
Mom and Dad told me.

What do you remember about my cancer?
Since I was a baby, I loved to play with my mom's hair with my fingers each day. When my mom's hair was gone, I couldn't do that anymore. Her hair is growing again, and I can play with it again.

What was the hardest part for you of my cancer?
When Mom got sick.

How was your teacher involved?
My teacher asked me a lot how my mom was doing.

What did you tell your peers?
I didn't tell my friends.

What advice would you give to other kids whose parents have cancer?
Give your parents lots of hugs and kisses.

Interview with Mari's Older Son
Age 12 (11 at diagnosis)

How did you find out about my cancer?
My dad and mom told me.

What do you remember about my cancer?
You slept on your spot on the sofa, curled up in a ball. You slept a lot. You and dad went to the appointments.

What was the hardest part for you of your mom's cancer?
It was hard to see you cry. It was also hard to see you so sad after Dad cut your hair.

How was your teacher involved?
My teacher regularly asked me how you were doing.

What did you tell your peers?
Two of my classmates have parents that had cancer. I told my friends that my mom had cancer, but she was going to be fine.

What helped you cope?
I just kept doing normal things. I kept playing baseball, swimming, and soccer. But I also gave my mom a lot of hugs and kisses each day. Tell your parents you love them each day.

What advice would you give to other kids?
I would tell them that the doctors and nurses will take care of your mom or dad. Do your best to help your parents with things around your house.

PART V
SURVIVORSHIP AND RESOURCES

Hope is the thing with feathers

that perches in the soul —

And sings the tunes without the words —

And never stops at all.

Emily Dickinson

14

CONNECTIONS AND CHANGES

Rhonda's Social Survivorship

A month after my final cancer treatment, I turned 40. I was eager to celebrate the dual milestones of turning 40 and being recently NED (No Evidence of Disease). I was happy to say goodbye to my 30s, grateful to have survived multiple medical mysteries and a difficult year of breast treatments. I was cautiously optimistic about my future and had no qualms about turning 40, having just faced my own mortality. Getting older is certainly better than the alternative.

In terms of my Big 4-0 soiree, six of my closest friends and I spent the weekend at a friend's cabin near Yosemite. We stayed at a large, three-story cabin nestled in the trees near a picturesque lake. We hiked among the trees, walked to the nearby lake, had facials in the hot tub, and ate and drank a ton. One friend led us in a yoga session on the balcony overlooking the trees. It was an incredible weekend of celebration and reconnection. However, when I returned from our mountain retreat, I learned that someone I had met at my children's art therapy class and kept in touch with had passed away. She died of stage 4 breast cancer that had metastasized to her brain. Sadly, she died on my 40th birthday and had a daughter my daughter's age, so her passing hit very close to home.

At the end of April, I had the good fortune of attending Camp Koru. Camp Koru (www.koruproject.com) is a week-long camp for young cancer survivors diagnosed between ages 18 and 39. It is touted as giving attendees the chance to "find healing and renewal through outdoor experiences in the ocean and mountains. Each alumni leader has returned to Camp Koru to lead and share their knowledge, experience, and inspiration with other survivors." I had the option of applying to learn surfing and stand-up paddle boarding in Hawaii, or skiing and snowboarding in Oregon. Without a doubt, I chose Hawaii. Camp Koru was an uplifting and rewarding experience, with an unexpected twist at the end. The campsite was on the beach, with ocean views from our cabin windows. The grounds were covered with plumeria trees, and white plumeria blossoms peppered the grounds. Two of my cabinmates were breast cancer survivors and the third was a brain cancer survivor. We wore matching Camp Koru rash guards and learned to surf in the magnificent waves alongside 15 young cancer survivors. We were all novice surfers and cheered on each other's successes. We also volunteered at a nature preserve, swam with sea turtles, and participated in campfire circle talks about our cancer experiences. We ate fresh, exquisite meals that showcased Hawaii's finest fruits and seafood. Rich in color and beautifully arranged, the food overflowed on our plates and nourished our bodies. At night, we talked about our experiences with cancer and answered personal, cancer-themed questions. The week culminated in a ceremony of us standing on the sea cliff receiving a necklace with the Camp Koru symbol. The waves crashed below our feet as we took pictures and rejoiced in our successes and growth.

Unfortunately, the last night of Camp Koru came with an unexpected twist. I was video chatting my family when I felt wetness on my dress near my chest. I hung up with them and discovered that I had a leak in my right radiated breast, near the incision line. I did not know if the implant itself was leaking or it was just body fluid. After the camp doctor examined me, she said that it was most likely just body fluid, but that I needed to contact my doctor. I emailed my doctor and was also on hold with the hospital during our final buffet dinner. I wanted to be present for the dinner, but I could not enjoy it because I was on hold and extremely worried. I did not know if I should go to the doctor in Hawaii or if it would even be safe to fly. Everyone around me was joyous and I was incredibly scared. My cabinmates checked on me, but I really wanted the support of my husband and family in California.

I flew home the next day and saw my oncologist and plastic surgeon. My plastic surgeon did not know if I had an infection and decided to do an implant exchange. My surgery was the day before my daughter's First Communion. I expected between 40 and 50 people at my house the next day for the First Communion party. My best friend drove up and helped me with the decorations and food. My chest was bandaged, and I was on pain medications. I wore a dress that fit over my bandages and had to take it easy while hosting the party. It was a challenging and harried experience, but I got through it and celebrated my daughter's special day among friends and family.

Another camp experience that I would highly recommend, which is for school-aged children and their families, is Camp Kesem (www.campkesem.org). Having a parent with cancer affects the entire family unit and alters the family dynamic in significant ways. Camp Kesem is "a nationwide community, driven by passionate college student leaders, that supports children through and beyond their parent's cancer. Kesem is the largest national organization dedicated to supporting children impacted by a parent's cancer, at no cost to families." Developed at Stanford in 2000,

Camp Kesem now has over 116 chapters in 42 states.

My children have been going to Camp Kesem in Northern California for four summers, twice through UC Davis, and twice through UC Berkeley. My family's first Camp Kesem event was a Camp Kesem Friends and Family day when I was still undergoing chemo. Set on a sprawling private ranch, the event stations included activities for kids, free massages for adults, a massive potluck, booths for other cancer-related programs, an area to write letters to campers, a flash mob dance, and much more. I was impressed by the organization and how much it offered. My children were accepted to camp that summer. At ages six and nine, they experienced their first time away from home (other than with grandparents). The camp was five nights and six days. We dropped our children off at a park, met their counselors and cabinmates, and loaded them on buses to go to the campsite. The camp provides typical activities such as swimming at the lake, ziplining, go-karts, and arts and crafts. The kids also have emotional support activities such as cabin chat, team circle and group songs. For the past four years, my children have had an invaluable camp experience with a sense of community and a boost of Kesem magic.

As a new survivor, I was able to make meaningful connections through celebrations with friends, Camp Koru, and Camp Kesem.

Another key component of my survivorship is honoring my cancerversary (the anniversary of a cancer diagnosis or completion of treatment). I believe that celebrating a cancerversary is important for survivors' emotional healing and recovery. March 13 has been a very important date in my life, marking the beginning of my cancer journey and the date of my last major surgery. I decided that I wanted to do something special on March 13 to flip the script on this date. Plus, my kids and I both had time off in the middle of March. I wanted to visit somewhere I had never been and that would be awe-inspiring. I decided to visit Paris and London with my family. On March 13, 2019, we visited the Eiffel Tower, the Arc de Triomphe, Musee d'Orsay, and the Louvre. I reflected on how different March 13 felt this year compared to the previous two years, transforming the date into something positive for myself and my family. Later that week, we visited Disneyland Paris, London, and the Making of Harry Potter. We made amazing family memories and reclaimed the date from one of dread and despair to one of hope and renewal. I decided that every March 13 from then I would celebrate, through traveling or other memorable ways.

On March 13, 2020, I celebrated my cancerversary again, this time in a small, 14-seater airplane above Nazca, Peru. My family and I (including my 81-year-old breast mother) flew over majestic, grandiose rock formations of iconic Peruvian symbols. March 13 was also the day that

President Trump issued the Proclamation on Declaring a National Emergency Concerning the Novel Coronavirus Disease (COVID-19) Outbreak. After a week of traveling through multiple cities and landscapes of Peru, I received an unexpected call from our travel agent. He said that the president of Peru was closing the borders in 24 hours and no one would be able to leave after that time due to a COVID-19 country-wide lockdown. We were more than eight hours away from Lima, which was the only way out of Peru by plane. The next morning, our day tour guide said that he would drive us to Arequipa. We tried to find flights from Arequipa to Lima, but there were none. The US Embassy was our only hope of leaving the country until the quarantine was lifted. We did not know how long we would be there because all flights both within and out of Peru were cancelled. Experiencing COVID-19 restrictions in Peru was quite an adventure. There was a heavy police and military presence on the streets. We were told that only one person could leave the hotel at a time. We spent three days in Arequipa, and then took a Peruvian Air Force plane to Lima. We were dropped near the airport at 7:15 PM, on the first night of Lima's 8:00 PM curfew. Uber was not responding, so after 30 minutes of tense waiting, a taxi driver picked us up. She drove us past more than eight military checkpoints, and we were stopped multiple times. We spent the next week in two hotels in Miraflores, a neighborhood in Lima. The first hotel was evacuated to make room for medical personnel treating COVID-19. My children and mother did not leave the second hotel. My husband and I left once a day to get food from the supermarket. All the restaurants were closed; only a few supermarkets and pharmacies were open. Everyone wore masks and waited in long single file lines to shop. After ten days, we received the much-anticipated phone call from the US Embassy that we were on the list to leave the next morning. We piled into a taxi, checked in outside of the Embassy, and took a long bus ride to the Air Force base next to the airport. We sat in makeshift rows in a hot airport hangar as military and airline personnel interviewed us, while military dogs sniffed our luggage. We landed in Washington DC at 2:00 AM and returned home at 9:00 PM. After two days of flying and airport sleeping, we were grateful to be home. It had been a very unusual but memorable cancerversary.

Nowadays, cancer is not on my mind nearly as often. I used to have the question of "Will the cancer come back?" intruding on my thoughts several times a day. It would pop up while I was in a meeting at work, or eating dinner with my kids, or attending a birthday party. Instead, what dances around my head is a more hopeful question, "Where will my family travel to, or what great experience will we have next March 13?"

A third key component of my survivorship is making lifestyle changes to improve my overall mental and physical health, and consequently reduce my risk of a breast cancer recurrence. In February of 2020, I joined a year-long clinical trial through Kaiser's Department of Lifestyle Medicine called Resilience Against Cancer (RACe). The focus of the study was helping breast cancer survivors improve health outcomes through whole food plant-based eating, regular exercise, and stress management. We were expected to log everything that we ate and drank for the first six months of the clinical trial. We also needed to log our daily exercise, water intake, and mindfulness activities. We reported our weight weekly and had weekly group sessions with the two instructors. We also had four sessions of one-on-one coaching around our food and exercise logs. This program was exactly what I was searching for to guide me in a healthier living paradigm shift.

We started sessions one month before COVID-19 restrictions began. I went to three classes in person before going to Peru; then the meetings switched to Zoom format for the rest of the study. Each week the presenters had a different topic, such as emotional eating, behavioral drift, mindfulness, food choices in restaurants, and much more. They provided us with Ted Talk links, peer-reviewed research articles, and other resources. We were able to increase our knowledge base on a wide range of health topics and relate them to our specific life experiences. I reset my body and made fundamental shifts in my exercise and eating habits. I am currently in the maintenance phase, which involves the second six months of the trial. It does not require daily monitoring, but still includes weekly weight checks and weekly support meetings with other graduates of the active phase.

Regarding food changes, I was able to limit meat easily, but seafood and dairy were another story. I love tuna, shrimp and salmon too much. I also can't say no to mussels, crab or lobster. I began drinking almond milk but am sometimes tempted by my family's regular milk. I increased my fruit and vegetable consumption and was able to eliminate many processed foods. We were also told to limit caffeine, so I switched to green tea. I added new foods into my diet, such as quinoa, chia seeds, zucchini noodles, and cauliflower rice. I also increased my consumption of tofu, beans, lentils, steel oats, and nuts. I moved the needle more toward whole foods, plant-based but still maintain a wide range of foods in my diet.

Regarding stress reduction and mindfulness, we have all had a much greater need for this due to COVID-19, and more time and opportunities for practice. I started watching yoga videos in the mornings and listening to mindfulness soundtracks before bed. I try to opt for long bubble baths with candles rather than a quick shower. I have learned to savor an oversized cup of tea. I started keeping a daily journal again and tried to include what I am grateful for each day.

In terms of exercise, I had trouble fitting this in when I was working full-time but did better after I started working from home due to COVID-19. Also, I was held accountable by my children, who logged their daily exercise minutes as part of their distance learning P.E. requirement. We exercised every day. Some of our favorite activities are bike riding, indoor dodgeball, swimming, and kayaking. I also purchased weights so I can work out at home.

To further boost my exercise routine and forge connections with cancer survivors, in June of 2020, I joined Triumph Fitness (www.triumphfound.org). Triumph provides free 12-week exercise programs designed specifically for recent adult cancer survivors, and has been around since 2005. The website notes that, "Participants are guided by cancer exercise specialists whose training certification enables them to understand the complex challenges survivors face. The program helps survivors regain strength, stamina, and confidence lost during their battles with cancer." Due to COVID-19, we were unable to meet in person for Triumph classes, which are typically held inside local gyms. Instead, we met only twice in person—during our initial class and graduation. That first day we met our instructors, shared cancer stories, and received workout equipment. They provided each participant with a high-quality yoga mat, four stretchy bands, long workout bands, a cloth stretching band, a door hinge, and a workout bag. We met on Zoom twice a week for 1 ½ hours each time. There were two instructors and ten participants. One instructor guided us verbally through the sequence of warm-up, cardio, strength training, cool-down, and meditation while the second instructor demonstrated the exercises. We pushed our limits and got a great workout, all in the comfort of our own homes. We were inspired to improve our fitness in a mindful, well-paced way.

In September, we met in person once again at the same spot where we met originally, to celebrate the completion of the program in an outdoor, socially distanced graduation. We took promotional pictures and videos among lily pads blowing in the wind. We wore masks and sat in a circle, while a film crew documented our final meeting. We shared our personal triumphs, especially during the isolating and difficult time of the COVID-19 pandemic. I was impressed by how much we had changed both physically and mentally in those three months, despite meeting on Zoom. It is amazing what people can attain when they put their minds to the accomplishment of a goal, especially in a supportive group setting. Cancer programs during COVID-19 presented difficult experiences and challenges, but we got through them together.

15

FAITH BEFORE FEAR

Jennifer's Spiritual Survivorship

My approach to survivorship is through a lens of spirituality and faith. People who are faced with a crisis can draw great strength from their spiritual background. I am sharing my spiritual guidance during my breast cancer journey so that it can be beneficial for others facing these challenges. I believe we are spiritual beings having an earthly or human experience. We all have challenges in life, and they come in different forms. It's up to us how we are going to respond and what we are going to learn from them. Stuart Scott, who died of cancer in 2015, gave an inspiring and insightful speech at the ESPY awards. He stated, "When you die, it does not mean that you lose to cancer. You beat cancer by how you live, why you live, and in the manner in which you live." This wise counsel can be applied to any struggle in life. I genuinely believe gratitude and faith help us in our responses to challenging times.

Gratitude is sometimes hard to express, especially amid our struggles. "No matter our circumstances, no matter our challenges or trials, there is something in each day to embrace and cherish. There is something in each day that can bring gratitude and joy if only we will see and appreciate it," said religious leader Dieter F. Uchtdorf. If we make a daily effort to have gratitude, we will be happier and have more strength to weather the storms. Keep a "gratitude journal" if you are struggling with feeling gratitude. Each day write about one thing you are thankful for; remember the simple things in life, things we tend to take for granted. "It is not happiness that brings us gratitude. It is gratitude that brings us happiness," according to a neuroscience study, "The Neuroscience of Gratitude and How It Affects Anxiety and Grief," published on Positivepsychology.com. This study states, "When we express gratitude and receive the same, our brain releases dopamine and serotonin, the two crucial neurotransmitters responsible for our emotions, and they make us feel 'good'. They enhance our mood immediately, making us feel happy from the inside." The greatest source of happiness is the ability to remain grateful in all circumstances.

During challenges we may question our faith;

questioning if we have enough faith. We may even be questioning if we have any faith left at all. Faith is not having a perfect knowledge of things; it is the assurance of things hoped for. In Hebrews 11:1 we read "Now faith is the substance of things hoped for . . ." Hope gives us courage to do those things that we don't believe we are capable of, and faith is a necessary foundation of hope. Faith and fear cannot coexist. We must not let our fears replace our faith. There may be times when you find yourself struggling to see how God is working in your life—times when you feel under siege—when the trials of this life bring you to your knees. Through His grace He will bless us and increase our capacity. He can give us eyes to see, even when it's hard. He can give us strength, even when we are tired or weary, and even when the outcomes are not as we hoped. Wait and trust in God and in His timing, because He sees the big picture and He has a plan for each of us. Remember, this earth life is just but a small moment in time compared to eternity. It is this faith that gives me hope, and that hope allows me to feel joy. Russell M. Nelson, President of the Church of Jesus Christ of Latter-day Saints, said, "The joy we feel has little to do with the circumstances of our lives and everything to do with the focus of our lives." Our joy depends on our focus. Personally, I strive to focus on my Lord and Savior and His gospel of hope. He is my one constant. When there is chaos around me, He offers me peace. So many times, I have been comforted, strengthened, or encouraged because of a prayer or silent plea for help. The times when I needed it the most, I was blessed with peace and stillness.

This same peace and stillness were given to my angelic friend Lucy, who passed away from breast cancer in August. I attended her COVID-19 safe memorial. It was held outside on beautiful temple grounds. I watched and listened in awe as her three amazing children and loving husband each spoke. Their profound love for Lucy was so apparent, as well as their deep faith. I was touched by their courage to walk God's plan. It was so comforting to know that they knew this separation was only temporary. Their comfort came from knowing they would see her again. Her husband stated so eloquently, "Lucy had enough faith to be healed, but she also had enough faith not to be healed."

My gratitude and faith have sustained me in my darkest hours and have helped me through my most difficult challenges. I have learned that I do not have control over a lot of things, but I do have control of how I respond to it all. I choose to have faith over fear. I choose to have hope and to live my best life despite my circumstances. May we all remain grateful and pray for courage to continue to walk God's plan. May we all live life with hope among us.

16

RESOURCES DURING TREATMENT

Breast cancer can be a very isolating and unsettling experience. It is important for people undergoing treatment to seek out resources – both in person and virtually. Below, Rhonda provides her top five resources she utilized during her treatment for breast cancer. She introduces each of the five resources in general and discusses how she benefited from them specifically. Her top five recommendations are: (1) meeting with cancer patients in local support groups or one-on-one, (2) joining online communities such as Breastcancer.org and Sharsheret.org, (3) arranging a cancer-friendly photography session, such as Magic Hour Foundation, and (4) finding a beauty program for cancer patients, such as Look Good Feel Better, and (5) scheduling massages tailored for cancer patients.

My first recommendation during treatment is meeting face-to-face with other breast cancer patients through support groups or one-on-one. While I am a private person, it helped me to connect emotionally with others in similar situations. I found a cancer support group when I enrolled my children in a free art therapy class at a local hospital. My kids met with other children whose parents had cancer or the children themselves had cancer. The class was led by an experienced art therapist who guided them through a different art lesson each week. At the same time, some of the parents met with a licensed psychologist and shared their experiences in a group therapy format. I connected with these women because we were all experiencing the struggles of cancer treatments while parenting young children.

I also met one-on-one for coffee chats with two women who were also undergoing treatment for breast cancer. One of the survivors, Raina, was the young woman who had given me the cooling caps. She texted me many times and guided me through some of the darker days, particularly right after chemo sessions and surgeries. She was very reassuring and provided me hope that there would be better days ahead, while also acknowledging the pain and difficulties of my current reality. When I met her, she had been diagnosed with triple positive breast cancer, and was in the middle of her year-long treatment of HER2+ chemotherapy. She is now healthy and NED (No Evidence of Disease). Amazingly, she became pregnant about a year after finishing chemo, and gave birth to healthy twins!

I was able to pay it forward and lend the cooling caps to someone who worked for the hospital. Perlita was diagnosed with triple negative breast cancer four months after me. We met for coffee several times and texted, as Raina had done for me. I passed on several books about cancer and other supplies to her. It helped both of us to compare our symptoms and commiserate with each other. I also visited her during one of her chemo treatments, as Raina had done for me. We still stay in contact and team up for the American Cancer Society's Making Strides Against Breast Cancer walk in Sacramento. She is doing well and is a peer navigator in the breast cancer survivorship program at our hospital!

My second highly recommended resource is the online breast cancer community. One site that I visited often is Breastcancer.org (www.breastcancer.org), a "nonprofit organization dedicated to informing and empowering individuals to protect their breast health and overcome the challenges of breast cancer." It is basically Facebook for breast cancer patients, but also includes articles and other resources. I started a profile for myself and searched for people who matched my statistics, such as living near me, having the same type of cancer, or undergoing the same treatments. I searched through threads and read about people's dilemmas in order to better inform my own decisions.

Another online breast cancer community I benefited from is Sharsheret (www.sharsheret.org). Sharsheret "is a Jewish breast cancer organization that helps women and their families face breast cancer." The website noted that "while our expertise is in young women and Jewish families as related to breast cancer and ovarian cancer, Sharsheret programs service all women and men." The organization provides a wide range of resources. I received support through their national Peer Support Network. My support person and I were matched in age, cancer type, and treatments. We talked several times, and she was able to really listen and understand what I was going through, while giving me helpful advice. I also received a care package for patients going through treatment, which included a folder, lotion, socks, inspirational cards, a candle, journal, and more. My children both received care packages which included coloring books, crayons, action figures, and journals. All of these gestures from Sharsheret uplifted our spirits and spread hope during the dark times.

My third resource is Magic Hour Foundation (www.magichour.org). Magic Hour Foundation is a non-profit agency and "national network of professional photographers who look to serve individuals and families fighting cancer. These charitable portrait sessions provide an opportunity for families to feel special and strong while they relax, smile and enjoy time with loved ones." I applied to the

Magic Hour Foundation while I was undergoing chemotherapy. I was matched with a photographer in our city. My hair was thinning from chemo and I was paler than usual, but I wanted to document this phase in my family's life. My mom joined us, and we color coordinated in light pink and grey. We met at a park near my house, and the photographer arranged us in various poses, combinations, and backgrounds. It turned out that she knew my husband, and our children attended the same school. She was also one of my daughter's troop leaders when Girl Scouts started a few weeks later! I received a beautiful box with our picture on the top containing printed pictures from the agency. I appreciate having that time in my life memorialized in pictures and still look at them to this day.

My fourth resource is the Look Good Feel Better program (www.lookgoodfeelbetter.org). This program provides in-person hair and makeup tutorials, and a complete makeup kit, to people going through cancer treatments. According to their website, "Look Good Feel Better is dedicated to improving the quality of life and self-esteem of people undergoing cancer treatment. The program offers complimentary group and virtual sessions that teach beauty techniques to help people with cancer to face their diagnosis with greater confidence." This program was my first cancer-related activity that I attended. I found an event that took place at my hospital. I was in a group with about eight other women and two presenters. They gave each of us a large bag of makeup that included name brand makeup, from foundation to brushes to lipsticks. As we applied the makeup to ourselves, the presenters gave general tips and special considerations for people undergoing treatment (such as how to pencil in eyebrows, avoid the sun, and tie head scarves).

My fifth and final recommendation is massage, preferably with a massage therapist certified to work with breast cancer patients. I received a free massage from a massage therapist at an event for cancer survivors (Camp Kesem Friends and Family Day). I contacted her afterwards and she offered to come to my house. Since she was getting her certification in massage therapy for cancer patients, she accrued hours and practice on me, while I benefited from in-home massages. She brought her own music and massage chair, documented my symptoms, and taught massage techniques to avoid lymphedema. While a professional in-home massage may not be practical, consider visiting a massage therapist who is certified for breast cancer patients.

Breast cancer treatments can be grueling. Beyond the support of my friends and family, community support helped carry me through my cancer treatments. However, each patient needs to tap into their particular resources of interest, and create a tailored support network that works for them. Additional community resources can be found at the comprehensive website, www.breastcancerfreebies.com.

17

FINAL THOUGHTS

Breast cancer has challenged the three authors in many ways but has also led to unexpected positive consequences. Cancer has broadened our connection to spirituality, commitment to health, appreciation of friends and families, and gratitude for life itself. Our families have been affected multiple times by a cancer diagnosis and we have emerged from the darkness more grateful and more informed. This journey has been filled with laughs, tears, anger, happiness, bravery, hopelessness, and in the end with hope.

All three of us are currently NED (No Evidence of Disease), but that status can change at any time, which is not taken lightly by any of us. We continue taking our anti-estrogen medication, having regular checkups with our oncologists, and doing follow-up scans as necessary. We try to manage scanxiety and fears of recurrence while maintaining gratitude and focusing on the many blessings in our lives.

Due to our diagnoses and history of breast cancer in our families, the critical importance of early detection of breast cancer in our children—a total of eight—cannot be overlooked. The current standard of care is for children of survivors to start screenings with mammograms ten years younger than the age that their mother was diagnosed.

As survivors and daughters of breast cancer survivors, we must also not ignore known or potential underlying genetic causes. Thankfully, Jennifer and Mari do not have any known genetic links to cancer. Due to Rhonda having a Variant of Uncertain Significance on her BRCA2 gene, she enrolled in a promising ongoing study, PROMPT: Prospective Registry of Multiplex Testing (www.promptstudy.info). According to their website, "PROMPT is an online research registry for people who have multiplex gene panels—a newer form of genetic testing that looks for mutations in several different genes at once. All genes on the panels have been linked to an increased risk of cancer, but some risks are better known than others." Rhonda supplied information about her and her relatives' cancer diagnoses, treatments, and genetic test results for their growing worldwide database. She gets periodic emails to update them with any changes to her or her family's health so they can track hereditary cancer risk.

We all support ongoing research and fundraising

around breast cancer. We been involved with various fundraising opportunities to promote breast cancer awareness and research in our community. Through the American Cancer Society (www.cancer.org), we have participated in annual walks, such as Relay for Life and Making Strides Against Breast Cancer. We bought coordinated pink and black baseball T-shirts and named our group the Sassy Survivors. We have also attended local breast cancer awareness events, such as those put on by Real Men Wear Pink of Sacramento. We are proponents of early detection of breast cancer through mammograms and ultrasounds.

Some basic tenets that have helped us thrive collectively as breast cancer survivors are: eat more whole foods and less processed foods; find what exercises you enjoy and do them more often; find ways to reduce your stress through meditation, yoga or other convenient outlets (especially during COVID-19); seek comfort in your spiritual beliefs and faith community; give back to the breast cancer community; celebrate your personal milestones (especially on your cancerversary); and find an outlet for your swirling thoughts (such as though journaling or poetry).

We strongly believe that laughter is a must, no matter how challenging or dark the days become. Laughing through the pain is an expression of hope. It's kind of this perspective of, "It'll all be okay in the end," so isn't humor a better way to approach things? Author Marjorie Pay Hinckley summed up the benefits of laugher by stating, "The only way to get through life is to laugh your way through it. You either have to laugh or cry. I prefer to laugh; crying gives me a headache."

Our most important piece of advice to other women going through this journey is to be kind to yourself. Tell yourself that you deserve grace and that your body and mind are going through things that nature does not normally do to you. You need time to process the magnitude of the journey you are going through. This is a big deal and whatever you are feeling right now is the correct feeling. Some days you will hate everyone and everything, while other days you will be happy and energetic. Some days you will want to be alone, while other days you will need support from family and friends. Some days you will feel hopeful, while other days you will feel hopeless. But the one thing that must remain constant is your resilience. You are so much stronger than you know. Breast cancer is an ongoing journey of struggles and triumphs, but there is hope among us.

RESOURCE WEBSITES

American Cancer Society
www.cancer.org

Breastcancer.org
www.breastcancer.org

Breast Cancer Action
www.bcaction.org

Breast Cancer Freebies
www.breastcancerfreebies.com

Camp Kesem
www.kesem.org

Camp Koru
www.koruproject.com

Look Good Feel Better
www.lookgoodfeelbetter.org

Magic Hour Foundation
www.magichour.org

Sharsheret
www.sharsheret.org

Prospective Registry of Multiplex Testing
www.promptstudy.info

Triumph Cancer Foundation
www.triumphfound.org

ACKNOWLEDGMENTS

First, and most of all, we are indebted to Claudia De Young, M.D., for guiding us through our breast cancer journeys and writing the foreword to this book. From biopsy to survivorship, Dr. De Young walked alongside us and was accessible through all stages of our breast cancer journeys. She informed us about standard treatments as well as holistic approaches to survivorship.

We would also like to express our deep appreciation to all the Kaiser Permanente staff. The infusion staff made personal connections with us through conversations, hugs, and check-ins, which were critical especially during COVID-19. The nursing staff assisted with relieving our anxiety and even decreasing our blood pressure by being compassionate and calming. We appreciate our oncologists, surgeons and cancer care teams who were proactive and thorough in reviewing our histories and providing us with comprehensive care.

Also, we owe a debt of gratitude to Aridai Morales at Intemporal Photography (www.intemporelbyam.com) for her astute eye in capturing our photos for this book. She also volunteers for Magic Hour Foundation (www.magichour.org)

and took Rhonda's timeless family portraits during chemo.

In addition, we want to acknowledge the staff at Camp Kesem (www.kesem.org) who work tirelessly to arrange week-long summer camps for children of cancer survivors. Jennifer and Rhonda are thankful that Camp Kesem provides ongoing support for their children and countless others, and builds a sense of community among college counselors, children and their families.

Furthermore, Rhonda gives special thanks to the Resilience Against Cancer (RACe) clinical trial staff, through the Department of Lifestyle Medicine at Kaiser Permanente, for guiding her in making fundamental behavioral shifts. John Camarillo and Jennifer Ledoux hosted six months of virtual meetings during COVID-19 and provided a wealth of information around whole food plant-based eating, exercise, and stress management.

Along those lines, Rhonda would also like to express her gratitude to Triumph Fitness (www.triumphfound.org) for their 12-week exercise program. With their expert coaching, Lisa Bauduin and Maria Gutierrez taught virtually during COVID-19 and helped cancer survivors transform their living spaces into gyms and transform their exercise routines.

Finally, we would like to thank our friends and family for supporting us throughout this journey. When faced with extreme challenges such as cancer and COVID-19, we are indeed stronger together.